ABERDEEN UNIVERSITY STUDIES
NUMBER 135

TRADE UNIONISM IN ABERDEEN

1878 TO 1900

Membership Certificate, Associated Shipwrights' Society,
Aberdeen (1893)

TRADE UNIONISM
IN ABERDEEN
1878 TO 1900

KENNETH D. BUCKLEY, B.A.(Lond.)

LECTURER IN ECONOMIC HISTORY, UNIVERSITY OF SYDNEY, N.S.W., AUSTRALIA
FORMERLY ASSISTANT LECTURER, UNIVERSITY OF ABERDEEN

Published for the University of Aberdeen by
OLIVER & BOYD
EDINBURGH: TWEEDDALE COURT
LONDON: 39A WELBECK STREET, W.1

FIRST PUBLISHED 1955

PRINTED IN GREAT BRITAIN AT
THE UNIVERSITY PRESS
ABERDEEN

PREFACE

THE investigations on which this book is based were carried out during my tenure of a lectureship at the University of Aberdeen. The valuable local material housed in the University Library at King's College and in the Public Library of the City provided the major part of the information. For the encouragement and facilities afforded to research by Aberdeen University, as well as for the financial sponsoring of the publication by the University, I wish to offer my sincere gratitude. In particular, I owe much to the stimulating and helpful advice of Professor H. Hamilton and Dr. E. M. Hampson of the Economics Department, and to Mr. J. Milne, secretary of the Aberdeen Trades Council, who did much to give me the atmosphere of the movement. My thanks are also due to the publishers for their meticulous care in printing.

K. D. BUCKLEY

DEPARTMENT OF ECONOMIC HISTORY
UNIVERSITY OF SYDNEY
N.S.W., AUSTRALIA
21st February, 1955

CONTENTS

PART I
THE ECONOMIC BACKGROUND

PART II
TRADE UNIONISM

PART III
ANALYSIS

PART IV
POLITICS

ILLUSTRATIONS

INTRODUCTION

IN the main, the period of time covered by this work is that of the Great Depression: a transitional period of malaise and ferment, of a searching for solutions to problems, old and new, amongst both workers and employers. It was one of the key periods of trade union history; for the first time on a permanent scale large numbers of unskilled workers became trade unionists, and many of the barriers between skilled and unskilled workers were broken down as class-consciousness developed. As Mr. Dobb says:

'Prior to this, the majority of the workers retained the marks of the earlier period of capitalism, alike in their habits and interests, the nature of the employment relation and the circumstances of their exploitation. Capacity for enduring organisation or long-sighted policies remained undeveloped; the horizon of interest was apt to be the trade and even the locality, rather than the class; and the survival of the individualist traditions of the artisan and the crafts-man, with the ambition to become himself a small employer, was for long an obstacle to any firm and widespread growth of trade unionism, let alone of class consciousness.'[1]

Associated with the rapid expansion of trade unionism was extraordinary political development: the re-birth of Socialism, a crisis in the Liberal party and the growth of independent Labour parties—in short, the origins of the modern Labour movement. In elections to local and national governmental bodies, more and more working-class organisa-tions insisted upon candidates from their own class, and, as a further development, upon the principle of independent Labour representation: the Bristol Labour League, formed by the Trades Council, put up a candidate for the School Board in 1886, in spite of Liberal appeals, and ran a can-didate for the Town Council the following year; three

[1] M. H. Dobb, *Studies in the Development of Capitalism* (1946), pp. 265-6.

Labour candidates were elected to the Newcastle School Board in 1888; the Hull Trades Council decided to contest a Town Council seat in 1890, and by January of the following year the Leicester Trades Council had returned two representatives to the Town Council and three to the School Board; in 1891, whilst there were formed the Labour Unions of Bradford, Huddersfield, and Colne Valley, the Salford Labour Electoral Association, and the (London) Labour Representation League, candidatures were being sponsored by the Trades Councils of Stockton, Leeds, and Hull, and the Carlisle Land and Labour League. In 1892 the *Workman's Times* provided a form of national co-ordination for these spontaneous and isolated movements, and Labour political organisations were formed in a number of other towns; the movement finally achieved a national organisation and leadership by the formation of the Independent Labour Party at the Bradford conference in January 1893.[1] Nevertheless, the period saw only the beginnings of an independent Labour political movement: in 1900 most workers were still Liberal or Conservative in political outlook.

From the point of view of Britain as a whole, numerous studies of such developments have been made; but there have been very few studies of regional development, and Scotland has been particularly neglected. This book attempts to fill that lacuna as far as one large Scottish city, Aberdeen, is concerned: it attempts to trace and analyse trade union expansion and the growth of a concept of independent Labour representation. The picture of trade unionism in Aberdeen which emerges—of changes in its dimensions, stature, social composition, and outlook—does not perhaps diverge startlingly from the national picture, but a close-up, on a local though detailed scale, may contribute to a better understanding of the processes generally at work at the time;

---

[1] For the local labour organisations, see D. W. Crowley, *The Origins of the Revolt of the British Labour Movement from Liberalism*, pp. 434-8 (unpublished Ph.D. dissertation, University Library, London); H. M. Pelling, *Origins and Early History of the I.L.P. 1880-1900*), pp. 90-1, *passim* (unpublished Ph.D. dissertation, University Library, Cambridge).

for example, in the case of Aberdeen, the key rôle played by skilled workers and the Trades Council.

As far as concerns the development of independent Labour representation—though it would be artificial to separate that from the general development of trade union-ism, since the two were part and parcel of the same process, with much the same leading personnel involved—Aberdeen was certainly no ordinary city. The Labour political move-ment in Scotland, at least in the larger industrial centres, seems to have been more advanced than in England: the Glasgow Trades Council participated in the first School Board election in 1873, and in 1879 the Edinburgh Trades Council ran working-men candidates for the School Board,[1] though in neither instance is it likely that these were actions taken independently of the Liberal party. Aberdeen was perhaps more advanced in this respect than any other area in Britain: as early as 1884, its Trades Council, acting independently of the Liberal party, secured the return of two working-men to the Town Council. Within a matter of ten years or so, the organised trade union movement, and a considerable proportion of the population, of Aberdeen turned away from Liberalism; and fortunately considerable material exists for the study of this swing of opinion, with its vacillations and tackings to and fro. This, then, is essentially a study of how Aberdeen became by the early eighteen-nineties 'a politically-phenomenal city . . . with a population of 120,000, with 7,000 organised workers, with a Socialist organisation which can dispose of hun-dreds of copies of a London paper at street corners in a week . . .'.[2]

Part One of the work gives a brief account of the more important industries in Aberdeen and of their varying importance and fortunes during the period. Part Two gives both a static and a dynamic picture of trade unionism; and

[1] Cf. W. H. Marwick, *Economic Developments in Victorian Scotland* (1936), pp. 201, 203.

[2] *The Workers' Herald*, 12 Dec. 1891 (in Aberdeen Public Library). The 'London paper' was probably *Justice*, organ of the S.D.F.

Part Three, by examining some economic and social factors, essays a partial explanation of the expansion of trade unionism. Part Four traces the movement of political and social thought and action away from Liberalism towards the standpoint of independent Labour.

PART I

THE ECONOMIC BACKGROUND

CHAPTER I

THE INDUSTRIAL STRUCTURE

IN the period under consideration, Aberdeen was a rapidly expanding city. There were changes in boundary which complicate estimates of population, but if the area of the city in 1901 be taken as a basis the population was 106,527 in 1881, 123,327 (estimated) in 1891 and 153,108 in 1901. These figures represent an annual percentage rate of increase (compound) of 1·48 in the decade 1881-91, and 2·19 in the decade 1891-1901, and may be compared with the rate of 1·75 in the decade 1871-81.[1]

The main industries of Aberdeen and the surrounding district were listed by the Aberdeen Chamber of Commerce in 1885, in a document submitted to a Royal Commission, as being 'spinning and manufacturing of wool, flax, hemp, and jute, spinning of cotton, manufacturing of paper, combs, soap, and candles, provision curing, granite stone dressing and polishing, shipbuilding and shipowning, engineering and ironfounding, fisheries, agriculture, and the industries dependent upon agriculture'[2]—to which may be added the building industry. A high proportion of the products of the manufacturing industries was exported, the extreme case being cotton yarn, the entire output of which went to India. Since this list of industries does not indicate their relative importance in the economy of Aberdeen, nor which industries were declining or expanding, some elaboration is desirable.

Taking the period as a whole, the granite industry and, allied with it, the building trades, comprised the most important group. In the 'eighties and more especially in the 'nineties, there was a rapid expansion of all branches of the

---

[1] *Daily Free Press*, 15 Sep. 1902; and see Census Reports.
[2] *Royal Commission on Depression of Trade and Industry*, 1886, First Report [C. 4621], p. 74.

3

granite industry: the architectural and monumental branch concerned with the preparation and polishing of granite blocks and monuments for such purposes as public works, tombstones, and columns; the settmaking branch engaged in the production of street setts and kerbs; and the building branch.[1] By 1900, compressed air rock-drills and steam-power were used for blasting and lifting operations in all the larger quarries, and the use of compressed air in stone-cutting had considerably reduced the cost of intricate carving and opened up a wide field for high-quality granite work; nevertheless, a great deal of cutting and polishing of granite was still done by hand, and the value of the highly-skilled stonemason was undiminished.[2]

The scale of business in the industry was small, and no large amount of capital was required to establish a manu-facturing yard. In 1884 it was estimated that there were between sixty and seventy firms of sculptors and polishers, employing about 1,400 men and boys, whereas there had been only three firms in the city twenty years earlier;[3] and a stonemasons' delegate to the Trades Council was com-plaining of systematic overtime, which 'particularly pre-vailed in the many small yards which had sprung up of late years'.[4] The extent and expansion of the industry are indicated in the Census Reports: there were 886 men and boys engaged in the monumental branch in Aberdeen in 1881, 1,290 in 1891, and 2,075 in 1901. The comparable figures for masons engaged in the building branch of the industry were 1,117 in 1881, 1,269 in 1891, and 1,504 in 1901.[5] Diack, himself a stonemason, claimed that in 1903

[1] For the organisation of granite manufacturing, see H. Hamilton, 'The Granite Industry' (Further Studies in Industrial Organisation, ed. M. P. Fogarty, 1948).
[2] H. Hamilton, loc. cit. p. 193; W. Diack, 'The Scottish Granite Industry' (The World's Work, Nov. 1903, pp. 635-8).
[3] Daily Free Press, 31 Dec. 1884.
[4] MS. Minutes, 30 July 1884, Aberdeen United Trades Council (in King's College Library, Aberdeen; hereafter referred to as Minutes).
[5] These Census figures include, in all cases, employers and self-employed, as well as employees. There was, of course, fluctuation in numbers, not brought out by the censuses, from one year to another.

9,000 people found employment in the granite industry in Aberdeenshire.[1]

The building industry, which in Aberdeen was very largely concerned with building in granite, was naturally closely connected with the granite industry, and experienced a comparable expansion in the 'nineties. There were, for example, about 620 carpenters and joiners in 1893,[2] when the building trades were busy, and perhaps 900 to 950 in 1900, a year of 'marked dullness' in the building trades.[3] Perhaps fortunately for the stonemasons, the two industries, building and granite, did not always share the same fortunes: notably so in 1894 when the monumental granite industry was going through a 'period of dullness' while the building trades showed 'uniform briskness', and many unemployed monumental masons consequently found employment in building.[4]

The most profitable industry, and the one which grew with the most startling rapidity in the two decades, was the white fish industry. Steam-trawling was introduced to the port in 1882; seven years later it had established itself firmly, and rapidly superseded the old line-fishing. Progress in the 'nineties was remarkable, especially after 1894 when the 'otter' trawl replaced the original beam trawl. In every year of the 'nineties, the catch of fish landed by steam trawlers and liners in Aberdeen increased substantially, both in weight and value; judged by both criteria, the catch doubled between 1889 and 1894, and doubled again between 1894 and 1900, the catch in the latter year being nearly 950,000 cwt., worth over £600,000. By 1902, when there were nearly 200 trawlers fishing from the city, Aberdeen had become the largest fishing port in Scotland, and the

[1] W. Diack, loc. cit. p. 633.

[2] Aberdeen Labour Elector, 18 Mar. 1893 (in King's College Library, Aberdeen).

[3] Daily Free Press, 15 Nov. 1900; 26 Dec. 1900. Census figures for 1891 and 1901, while confirming the impression of expansion, show that a considerably larger number of people (e.g. 1,464 in 1901) were classed as carpenters and joiners. As in the granite industry, however, the scale of business in carpentry was small, and the number of employers and self-employed persons correspondingly large.   [4] Ibid. 25 Dec. 1894.

third largest in the United Kingdom. As trawl-fishing
concentrated on Aberdeen, with its fine harbour, market,
and railway facilities, so the fishing villages of the north-east
coast of Scotland fell into decline; some of their inhabitants
turned to herring-drifting, others moved into Aberdeen.[1]

Fishing itself was by no means the whole story. Based
upon fishing, there grew up a number of subsidiary industries such as fish-curing, box-making, and ice-manu-
facture.[2] Between 1886 and 1891, three ice-making factories
were established in Aberdeen, and in the 'nineties there was
a very large growth of timber imports from Scandinavia,
mainly for the manufacture of fish boxes and barrels in the
city. Pyper estimated that in 1903 there were about 1,700
trawl fishermen,[3] 710 salesmen and labourers in the fish
market, and 1,100 people engaged in the curing of white
fish—a total of 3,510, to which he added about 1,500 men
and boys employed in the building and repairing of trawlers.
Undoubtedly, the fishing industry was a major factor in the
expansion and prosperity of Aberdeen in the 'nineties, and by
the end of the decade it was a strong rival to the position of
the granite industry as the most important industry in the city.

The fishing industry, with its demand for trawlers, was
the salvation of shipbuilding in Aberdeen. Shipbuilding in
the port had a long and, in the era of the clippers, a great
tradition; but the 'seventies, when the use of iron, and to
some extent steel, replaced wood in British shipyards, were
difficult years for local firms. Aberdeen, distant from supplies
of iron and steel and coal, and therefore faced with heavy
transport costs, was in no position to compete with the Clyde
and the Tyne in the building of large ocean-going vessels.
Only the three largest shipbuilding firms survived the

---

[1] H. Hamilton, 'The White Fish Industry in Aberdeen', pp. 108-9 (*Further Studies in Industrial Organisation*, ed. M. P. Fogarty); W. Pyper and others, *History of a Great Industry* (pamphlet, Dundee, 1903). See Appendix, Table I.
[2] H. C. McKenzie, *Third Statistical Account: The City of Aberdeen* (1953), pp. 177-8.
[3] W. Pyper, *op. cit.* p. 25. Almost certainly a serious over-estimate. According to the census of 1901, there were 976 fishermen in Aberdeen, of whom 22 were employers and 309 worked on their own account.

'seventies and one of these, John Duthie, Sons and Co., was forced to close down temporarily in the late 'seventies, re-opening in 1882. In the 'eighties and 'nineties, the industry tended to stagnate, suffering periodic and prolonged bouts of depression; the number of people employed by the three firms showed little or no tendency to increase, being about 2,000 to 2,500 in good years and considerably less in periods of depression.[1]

The shipbuilding industry was saved from extinction by the prosperity of fishing. The first Aberdeen-built steam trawler was launched in 1883, and from then onwards the shipbuilders increasingly specialised in trawler design and production. In 1899, a good year for the shipbuilding industry, twenty-six out of twenty-eight vessels launched in Aberdeen were trawlers;[2] between 1883 and 1903 a total of 267 trawlers was built by the three local firms.[3]

Besides the marine engineering plants associated with the shipbuilding industry, there was a fairly extensive general engineering and ironfounding industry in the city. In the main, these firms were concerned with making agricultural and stone-working machinery, catering for the local agricultural and granite industries.

Judged by the number of people employed—a rather deceptive pointer in this case—the textile industry was still of great importance to Aberdeen. Nearly all branches of manufacture were represented: the Broadford linen factory, customarily employing well over 1,000 people; the Grand-holm woollen and the Gordons Mills carpet-weaving factories; the Bannermill cotton-spinning works; the Aberdeen Jute Company. These were all large concerns, employing mainly women, and there were also several smaller hosiery factories; in all, about 6,000 people were employed in textiles in 1888.[4] For the greater part of the 'eighties and 'nineties, however, these textile firms were in difficulties of one kind or another, attributable in large measure to their dependence upon exports. Increased American tariffs

---

[1] H. C. McKenzie, *op. cit.* pp. 263-4. [2] *Daily Free Press*, 27 Dec. 1899.
[3] W. Pyper, *op. cit.* p. 25. [4] *Daily Free Press*, 27 Dec. 1888.

affected exports of woollen goods;[1] near-famine conditions
in India affected the export of cotton yarn in 1895-6 and
1899-1900 (the Bannermill usually exported its whole
output to India, though in these difficult years it was able,
by way of partial compensation, to find some outlet in the
Glasgow market);[2] and fluctuations of exchange, as between
countries having a gold and those having a silver standard
of value, added their quota of difficulties.[3] Labour relations
in the textile factories were extraordinarily embittered, and
were not improved by instances of victimisation of trade
unionists; in the 'eighties there was strike after strike, mainly
against reductions of wages, and a further crop of strikes in
the late 'nineties. That the general effect of all these difficulties was to weaken the position of the local firms is
strongly suggested by the fact that the Broadford linen works
closed down in 1898, re-opening some months later after
financial reconstruction, and that a few years later, in 1904,
the Bannermill and Gordons Mills closed down permanently.

Quite otherwise was the condition of the paper-making
industry in the period. There were four paper mills in
Aberdeenshire, employing about 2,500 people in 1886;[4] a
fifth mill was opened two years later. Strictly speaking, only
one of these mills was situated within the city, but three of
the others were closely connected with Aberdeen for such
matters as labour supply, and made a marked contribution
to its economy. The industry throve, and between 1886 and
1900 the annual trade reports on it in the *Daily Free Press*
abound in such terms as 'eminently satisfactory', 'very
prosperous', 'one of the most prosperous of local industries',
and 'vigorous'. Indeed, probably from the nature of its
products, such as newsprint and wrapping-paper, the

---

[1] *Daily Free Press*, 30 Dec. 1891; 28 Dec. 1896.

[2] *Ibid.* 27 Dec. 1895; 27 Dec. 1900.

[3] *Royal Commission on Depression of Trade and Industry*, 1886, First Report
[C. 4621], p. 74. In 1896, the manager of the Bannermill arranged for W. H.
Drew, of Bradford, a representative of the Bi-Metallic League, to address the
Trades Council. The Council, after due consideration, decided against the
principle of bi-metallism, on the grounds that it 'simply meant protecting
certain industries to detriment of other industries' (*Minutes*, 5 Feb. 1896;
23 June 1897; 11 Aug. 1897).   [4] *Daily Free Press*, 25 Dec. 1886.

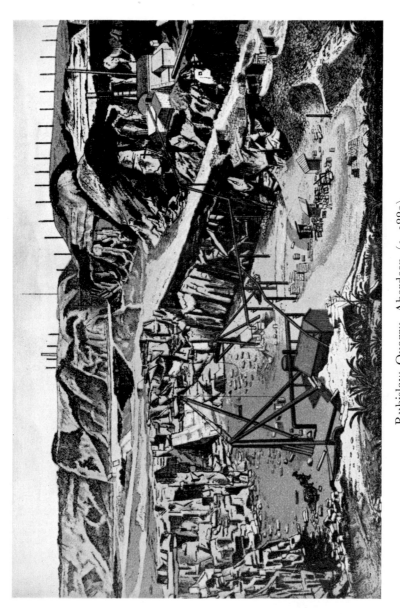

Rubislaw Quarry, Aberdeen (c. 1880)

Grandholm Woollen Mills, Aberdeen (1875)

industry seems to have been relatively immune from depression: it suffered severely in only one year, 1892, when it was feeling the effects of the American McKinley tariff.[1]

Lastly, amongst the industries of Aberdeen there may be noted the two comb-making firms. These do not seem to have been very prosperous in the two decades; but in 1899, when they employed 1,160 people, they amalgamated, together with a third and smaller firm in York, to form the Aberdeen Comb Works Company Ltd. The York factory was closed, and the company then controlled considerably more than 90 per cent. of the total production in the United Kingdom of horn combs.[2]

Two things are immediately apparent from this rapid survey of the more important industries in Aberdeen: their variety, and the relative lack of heavy industry. These characteristics are of considerable importance in considering economic fluctuation in the city. Yet if there was variety, there was also a pattern as well as considerable interdependence: with the exception of paper-making, all industries of importance stemmed from agriculture,[3] granite, or fishing. As will be seen in greater detail, the positions in the period of the granite and building industries on the one hand, and of the shipbuilding and engineering industries on the other, were in marked contrast to one another, particularly so far as employment was concerned.

[1] *Daily Free Press*, 31 Dec. 1892. See H. C. McKenzie, *op. cit.* pp. 273 *et seq.* for the local paper industry generally.

[2] H. W. Macrosty, *The Trust Movement in British Industry* (1907), p. 326.

[3] Except in so far as the labour-market was concerned, no attention is here devoted to agriculture, but it should be remembered that Aberdeen was the main market for a very wide agricultural area—a countryside which was seriously depressed in the early 'eighties, when Aberdeenshire farmers were agitating on a large scale for rent abatements and reform of the land-laws (e.g. see *Daily Free Press*, 13 Sep. 1881), but which, with its emphasis on meat production, was generally less severely affected by depression in the 'eighties and 'nineties than were most other agricultural districts of Britain—as, for example, in 1893 (*Daily Free Press*, 29 Dec. 1893). The demands of agriculture, and the by-products supplied by it, were responsible for the existence in Aberdeen of a number of subsidiary industries, such as engineering and chemical works, food-preserving and tinplate works, and the manufacturing of boots and shoes, soap, candles, and horn combs.

2 *

ECONOMIC FLUCTUATIONS

IT is not to be expected that economic development in Aberdeen would be directly at variance with national development in the last two decades of the nineteenth century, nor that the city would be exempt from the operation of the national trade cycle. Speaking very broadly, Aberdeen experienced a slump in the years 1878-9, followed by a short burst of revived activity in 1880-3. Depression conditions recurred from 1884 to 1887, to be succeeded by a boom from 1887-8 to 1891; 1892 to 1894-5 were years of heavy depression, but were followed by a period of expanding trade and industry from 1895 to 1900.[1] Nevertheless, this apparent conformity to the national pattern cloaks some very important divergencies from it.

In the first place, as observers remarked, Aberdeen was 'about the last of the large cities in the country to suffer by general backwardness of trade . . . equally true that it is about the last to feel the quickening of revival'.[2] Certainly in the 'seventies and 'eighties there was some truth in the remark: in the depression of 1878-9, the Aberdeen members of the Boilermakers, Iron and Steel Shipbuilders' Society received no unemployment assistance from their society— the available funds had been exhausted by members farther south before the slump reached Aberdeen;[3] the wages of agricultural workers in the north-east of Scotland tended to lag some two years behind the fluctuations in wages of agricultural workers in Great Britain;[4] and the time-lag may account for the fact that the Aberdeen Chamber of

---

[1] The terms 'boom' and 'slump' are, of course, used relatively and refer particularly to the employment position. Total production, in Aberdeen as in Britain, continued to expand over the period as a whole.

[2] *Daily Free Press*, 30 Dec. 1885.   [3] *Ibid.* 24 Dec. 1885.

[4] R. Molland and G. Evans, 'Scottish Farm Wages from 1870 to 1900' (*Journal Royal Statist. Soc.*, vol. CXIII, 1950, p. 225).

Commerce dated the fall in the rate of profit in industry, characteristic of the period of the Great Depression, from as late as 1881,[1] some time later than the phenomenon made itself apparent in the rest of Britain.

Secondly, and more important, Aberdeen suffered from depression less severely than other industrial centres. This is best illustrated by an examination of the major phases of economic fluctuation.

The slump of 1878-9 hit Aberdeen hard, the shipbuilding and building industries being particularly depressed. Repeated and extensive reductions of wages were imposed upon masons, joiners, boilermakers, and others, the boilermakers' reduction being as much as 17 per cent., and a number of unsuccessful strikes followed, the joiners', for example, being broken by a large influx of men from the west of Scotland where the crash of the City of Glasgow bank had caused widespread distress.[2] In the two and a half years from 1878 to mid-1880, the 210 members of the Aberdeen branch of the Boilermakers' Society were unemployed for an average of twenty-three weeks each.[3]

Recovery came in 1880, and for three or four years employment was high, shipbuilding being exceptionally active in 1883, when more than 11,000 tons were launched.[4] In these years also increases in wages were obtained in the shipbuilding industry locally.

For Britain as a whole, the years 1884-7 were probably the worst continuous sequence, from the point of view of unemployment, of any in the last quarter of the century; for 1887, for example, the trade union figures indicate 10·2 per cent. unemployment in the engineering, shipbuilding, and metal trades, and 8·2 per cent. in the building trades.[5]

---

[1] *Royal Commission on Depression of Trade and Industry*, 1886, First Report [C. 4621], p. 74. Complaints of keen competition and reduced profits came from nearly all industries in Aberdeen in the 'eighties and early 'nineties.

[2] *Minutes*, 6 Nov. 1878; 26 Feb. 1879.

[3] *Daily Free Press*, 24 Dec. 1885.

[4] See Appendix, Table II, for shipbuilding output.

[5] W. Rostow, *British Economy of the Nineteenth Century* (1948), p. 49; J. H. Clapham, *Economic History of Modern Britain*, vol. III (1938), p. 6, footnote.

Aberdeen, by comparison, escaped relatively lightly, though there was much unemployment and distress in the city. Shipbuilding was the industry worst affected. In 1884, there was heavy unemployment amongst shipbuilding workers, and considerable reductions in wages for those who retained their employment: Hall, Russell and Co., the largest firm, was reported to be employing only 650 workers at the end of the year, half the number employed the year before; J. Duthie, Sons and Co. had only one-quarter of their usual number of workers; whilst the third firm, Hall and Co., managed to keep on their 400 employees.[1] The engineering industry, apart from its marine branch, was not as yet affected. In the following year the depression deepened. The engineering and ironfounding industry was now affected, and hundreds of engineers were unemployed. It was estimated that in the shipbuilding and allied industries the number of men employed was about one-half the number for a good year.[2] Mackintosh, one of the boilermakers' delegates to the Trades Council, gave precise figures of unemployment in the Aberdeen branch of the society: the branch had 279 members, 210 of whom were unemployed at some time between 1 January 1884 and 21 December 1885; over the two years, these 210 men had been unemployed for an average of 22·2 weeks each, and the branch had paid out £1,084 5s. 2d. in unemployment benefit, together with £351 18s. 2d. in sick and special benefit.[3]

In 1886, when the new tonnage launched was less than 2,000, the shipbuilding industry 'practically collapsed', and engineering experienced 'extreme dullness'; wages of iron-shipbuilders and iron-moulders were reduced; it was thought that at least 75 per cent. of the iron-shipbuilders were unemployed, and much the same was true of the shipwrights; one-third to one-half of the moulders were unemployed; and the blacksmiths in the city were unemployed for an average of seven weeks each during the year.

---

[1] *Daily Free Press*, 25 Dec. 1884.   [2] *Ibid*. 30 Dec. 1885.
[3] *Ibid*. 24 Dec. 1885. The national figure of unemployment amongst boilermakers, 1884-7, was 20·3 per cent.

Towards the end of the following year, however, a revival began in shipbuilding and engineering, and the worst was over.[1]

But if the shipbuilding side of the picture was black the same could certainly not be said of the building and granite industries in Aberdeen in these years. In 1884, the building industry was not affected by depression, and the amount of housebuilding during the year was 'nothing less than marvellous'; the granite industry was, on the whole, 'as busy as in 1883'.[2] For granite manufacturers, 1885 was 'fairly good', though there was some unemployment and short-time working towards the end of the year; the two years which followed were better. Similarly, the building trades found 'sufficient if not abundant work' during the greater part of 1885, were 'without forward bound, but active' in 1886, and 'brisk' in the following year; there was some unemployment amongst joiners in 1885-6, but little amongst masons.[3]

Of the other local industries in these years, there was relatively little unemployment in textiles, though there were 5 per cent. wage-cuts in the linen, cotton, and jute factories in 1885-6; paper-making was 'vigorous' and 'rather above an average' in 1886 and 1887; shipping and the harbour trade, naturally affected by the general depression, were inactive and 'flat'; and herring fishing was depressed.

Without glossing over the evidence of unemployment, reduced wages, and social distress, the general conclusion is inescapable: Aberdeen came out of the depression of the mid-'eighties relatively well, partly as a result of the variety of its industries, mainly as a result of the strength of the monumental granite industry—which contemporaries attributed largely to the virtually monopolistic position of the local industry—and of the associated building trades. As the *Daily Free Press* said later, in referring to the monumental branch of the granite trade, 'It is now a familiar story that

[1] *Daily Free Press*, 25 Dec. 1886; 27 Dec. 1887.
[2] *Ibid.* 25 Dec. 1884; 31 Dec. 1884.
[3] *Ibid.* 30 Dec. 1885; 25 Dec. 1886; 27 Dec. 1887. See Appendix, Table III.

throughout the recent memorable period of trade depression it stood almost unaffected'.[1] 'While every other important centre suffered heavily amid the recent industrial depression, Aberdeen escaped to a great extent, owing almost entirely to its dependence on granite manufactures.'[2] There is perhaps an element of exaggeration in this last-quoted statement, but the workers, on their side, were no less aware that conditions elsewhere were worse. At a meeting on 24 December 1884, the Aberdeen Trades Council considered the draft of a letter to be sent to the Glasgow Trades Council in reply to one from that body concerning the depression and its causes:

'With regard to trade in our own city, we believe the trade here is not in so depressed a condition as it is in many of the centres of commerce. This city, in fact, is less affected than most other places owing to the great variety of our industries. None of our factories are closed, although orders are scarce. The shipping and kindred trades are affected to the greatest extent. . . . The greatest evils with which we have to contend arise from or are exaggerated by the action of our land laws as at present framed, throwing as they do the burden of taxation on industry generally, and most severely on the operative classes. . . .'[3] The draft was approved with the addition of a phrase suggested by an ironmoulders' delegate with a rather narrower, more practical turn of mind: 'That the systematic working of overtime, in the opinion of the Council contributes largely to bring about depression in trade.'[4]

The signs of general trade revival which had been apparent in Aberdeen in the latter part of 1887 became more marked in the following year; this was particularly

[1] *Daily Free Press*, 30 Dec. 1890.   [2] *Ibid.* 27 Dec. 1887.
[3] Quoted in *Daily Free Press*, 25 Dec. 1884. The attribution of depression to the land-laws is a good illustration of the strength of the Radical crofting agitation in Scotland in the 'eighties: Arthur O'Connor, the lone signatory to a minority report of the Royal Commission on Depression of Trade and Industry, 1886, in which he considered the depression to be due mainly to exorbitant rents, was less of an Irish voice in the wilderness than one might suppose.   [4] *Minutes*, 24 Dec. 1884.

so in the case of shipbuilding, although there was some tapering-off in activity in the building trades. 1889-90 were years of exceptional economic activity in nearly all industries; extensive house-building went on, more than 9,000 tons of shipping were launched in each year, and the monumental granite industry frantically boosted exports to the U.S.A. to get them in under the threatened McKinley tariff.[1] 1891 was not too bad a year: there was unemployment amongst monumental masons in the latter part of it, and imports of foreign granite had their effect on the quarrying side of the industry; but the building trades were 'fully more prosperous' than in the previous year, and the engineering industry was very busy, although the shadow of coming depression could be seen plainly in shipbuilding by the end of the year.[2]

Depression was back again in the years 1892-5. This time the granite industry did not escape, but again it was shipbuilding which bore the brunt. By December 1892, many shipbuilding workers were unemployed—the largest firm alone had paid off nearly 150 men—and most of the remainder were to be put upon short-time; engineering maintained a fair degree of activity. In 1893, shipbuilding touched bottom, with launchings of less than 3,000 tons, though there was some improvement on this in the following year; engineering was now affected, especially in the 'local' branches producing marine engines and granite-polishing machinery, and the Footdee Iron Works, employing about 100 men, virtually closed down. Meanwhile, the monumental granite industry, which had had a 'year of very fair prosperity' in 1892, was in a depressed condition by the latter part of 1893, and remained 'dull', with considerable unemployment amongst the granite cutters, in the following

[1] *Daily Free Press*, 27 Dec. 1888; 31 Dec. 1889; 30 Dec. 1890. The McKinley tariff came into effect in October 1890, and increased the import duty on manufactured granite from 20 per cent. to 40 per cent. Nevertheless, exports of Aberdeen granite to the U.S.A. in 1891, though naturally lower than in 1890, were still well above the 1889 level. The Wilson tariff of August 1894 reduced the U.S. import duty on granite by 10 per cent.

[2] *Ibid.* 23 Dec. 1891; 29 Dec. 1891; 30 Dec. 1891.

year; granite quarrying was naturally affected; and sett-making was depressed throughout these years, when wood was being adopted in many large cities of the south as a less noisy material than granite setts for roadmaking. The branches of the textile industry were subject to considerable fluctuation, the jute-workers, for example, being put on a forty-, in place of the usual fifty-six-, hour week in 1893.[1]

On the other hand, the building trades were far from being in a depressed condition. In building activity in Britain as a whole, 'the 'nineties show the greatest activity of any recorded decade',[2] and Aberdeen was no exception. Between 1890 and 1899, there was a long building boom in the city, when 'streets of new granite houses were being built by speculative builders on all sides. These were rapidly filled by thousands who drifted in from the small stagnant northern burghs'.[3] The Town Council made a small contribution by building its first housing estate in 1896. Moreover, this extraordinary building activity in the 'nineties had been preceded by a continuous period of active building from 1883, and that in turn by a building boom from 1870 to 1876-7: in the last three decades of the century building contractors were catering on a large scale, for the first time, for the needs of the working-classes in the city, and block after block of tenements was run up.[4]

[1] *Daily Free Press*, 22 Dec. 1892; 29 Dec. 1892; 30 Dec. 1892; 31 Dec. 1892; 25 Dec. 1893; 28 Dec. 1893; 29 Dec. 1893; 13 Dec. 1894; 25 Dec. 1894; 26 Dec. 1894.

[2] J. H. Clapham, *op. cit.* vol. III, p. 30. In no single year of the decade was recorded unemployment amongst carpenters and joiners higher than 4·4 per cent.

[3] J. Leatham, 'Sixty Years of World-Mending ', *The Gateway*, vol. XXIX, no. 343 (1941), p. 14.

[4] House-building activity in Aberdeen in the 'eighties (see Appendix, Table III), with its stimulus to the granite industry, is not easy to explain in relation to the moderate rate of increase of population in the decade. It is probably partly attributable to a rising standard of living from the mid-'eighties, but that does not go far towards explaining the sharp contrast with the lack of similar building in Glasgow (cf. A. K. Cairncross, 'The Glasgow Building Industry, 1870-1914', *Review of Economic Studies*, vol. II, 1934-5). According to the *Daily Free Press*, 26 Oct. 1888, 'accommodation has been provided for an increase of population far beyond the requirements of the town . . . the result being that to all appearance the property market has

Aberdeen Trawlers (1881)

PAPER WORKS AT CULTER 1850

Culter Paper Works, Aberdeen (1850)

The building industry was virtually unaffected by the depression of the early 'nineties; 1894, for example, was a year of 'uniform briskness' in the building trades, and many unemployed monumental masons were absorbed into building work.[1] The boom reached its height during the years 1896-9, and then ended quite suddenly in the closing months of 1899, when the rate of interest was high, and 'more than an impression is abroad that in some quarters of the city at least something like over-building has been going on, and a decline in the value of house property may ensue'.[2]

In the later years of the 'nineties, building was far from being the only industry which prospered. By the latter part of 1895, the general depression in the city was clearly lifting. Even the shipbuilding industry, though still in the doldrums (the Trades Council petitioned unsuccessfully for Aberdeen to be put on the Admiralty list for naval construction[3]), was now beginning to feel the beneficial effects of the great prosperity of the fishing industry.[4] General revival continued and expanded in the following year, the granite industry being 'very prosperous'.[5] 1897 and 1898

become seriously glutted. . . . It was not need therefore, that induced the speculation in house building; a too easy money market has been at the bottom of a great deal of the mischief. . . . Remunerative investments are exceedingly difficult to find; limited liability companies are at a discount just now; and investors have been flying to house property as a supposed good security for their spare cash. . . .'

[1] *Daily Free Press*, 25 Dec. 1894.

[2] *Ibid.* 26 Dec. 1899. There are indications that house rents had been 'sticky' over the two decades: the Trades Council agitated, in 1886, for courts to fix 'fair' house rents (*Minutes*, 3 Mar. 1886; 31 Mar. 1886); the building boom of the 'nineties developed in spite of the fact that in 1893 there were nearly 1,000 unoccupied houses with (average?) rentals of less than £7 per year (*Minutes*, 12 April 1893); and in 1898 there were complaints of a recent 'unnecessary rise in rents' (*Minutes*, 6 April 1898). There were also complaints of jerry-building (*Minutes*, 22 Mar. 1899).

[3] *Minutes*, 24 April 1895. The Council was not entirely logical in this: six years earlier, it had resolved 'That this Council protests against the excessive expenditure of 21½ Millions for naval purposes as being uncalled for and a gross injustice and hardship to the British taxpayer' (*Minutes*, 27 Mar. 1889).

[4] *Daily Free Press*, 26 Dec. 1895; 27 Dec. 1895.

[5] *Ibid.* 26 Dec. 1896; 28 Dec. 1896.

were remarkably good years for nearly all industries.[1] In particular, it may be noted that the granite industry maintained 'great prosperity' in spite of 'an enormous fall' in exports to the United States: in the years following 1894, when a similar situation had produced a depression in the Aberdeen industry, alternative markets had been found at home and abroad.[2] The shipbuilding industry was in the unusual position of being able to register 'exceptional briskness'. The textile firms were the only ones not doing exceptionally well.

The last two years of the period, 1899 and 1900, were still good for most industries—though with a tendency for economic activity to taper off—especially for shipbuilding and fishing; by the latter year, however, there was 'marked dullness' in the building trades, and considerable unemployment amongst masons.[3]

[1] *Daily Free Press*, 24 Dec. 1897; 25 Dec. 1897; 28 Dec. 1897; 27 Dec. 1898; 28 Dec. 1898; 31 Dec. 1898.

[2] 'The fall in the American trade has had the effect of concentrating the attention of Aberdeen [granite] merchants on the English markets' (*Daily Free Press*, 25 Dec. 1894). It had been noted in the late 'eighties that 'A very satisfactory feature of the [monumental] trade is the improving tendency that exists in the south in favour of employing dressed and carved granite for the front of banks and other imposing structures' (*Daily Free Press*, 27 Dec. 1888).

[3] *Daily Free Press*, 27 Dec. 1899; 28 Dec. 1899; 29 Dec. 1899; 15 Nov. 1900; 11 Dec. 1900; 26 Dec. 1900; 27 Dec. 1900.

PART II

TRADE UNIONISM

A GENERAL VIEW

BEFORE attempting to give a dynamic picture of the development of trade unionism in Aberdeen in the 'eighties and 'nineties, it is worthwhile considering the level of trade union organisation locally from a more general point of view. In such consideration the type, structure, and vicissitudes of the industries already outlined are of importance, and set the general framework within which trade unionism might develop—as also did the national position of trade unions in a particular industry. Needless to say, such a relation of trade unionism to the structure of industry cannot be treated mechanically: the policy and activity of a particular trade union or branch of a trade union are also of primary importance in determining its strength. A simple illustration of that may be given from the local strike of carpenters and joiners against an attempt by their employers to reduce wages in 1893-4: the strike, which lasted for nine weeks, was successful, and as a result the Aberdeen branches of the carpenters' and joiners' unions were considerably strengthened.[1] Nevertheless, even in this case, when all allowance has been made for the determination and solidarity of the carpenters, the success of the strike cannot be entirely dissociated from the fact that the building industry was not going through a period of depression at the time.

As might be expected, stable branches of national craft unions (British or Scottish) existed throughout the period in the shipbuilding and metal-working industries—the Boilermakers' Society, the Associated Society of Shipwrights, the Amalgamated Society of Engineers, the Associated Society of Ironmoulders of Scotland, and the (Scottish) Associated Blacksmiths' Society. Similarly in the

[1] *Minutes*, 14 Feb. 1894.

building industry there were branches of two carpenters' and joiners' societies, the Amalgamated and the (mainly Scottish) Associated, and of the United Operative Plumbers' Association; and a local union of slaters, which joined the Amalgamated Slaters' Society of Scotland in 1892. In the late 'eighties and early 'nineties there was a burgeoning of craft unions in the building trades, branches being formed of the Scottish National Operative Plasterers' Federal Union, and of the Scottish National Federation of House and Ship Painters; whilst the masons, whose organisation had lapsed for a few years, formed a strong local union, the Aberdeen Operative Masons' and Stonecutters' Union. Indeed, the reflection in trade unionism of the expansion of building and relative decline of shipbuilding was marked: the building craft unions played an increasingly important part in the Trades Council, whilst the shipbuilding and engineering unions, which had been the mainstay of the Council in the late 'seventies and early 'eighties, tended to fall into the background—so much so that for several years in the 'nineties, for no apparent reason, the boilermakers and the engineers were not affiliated to the Trades Council.[1]

Superficially, the textile and paper-making mills, with their large aggregations of workers, might seem to have provided a promising field for trade union organisation, but such was not the case. The textile workers were mostly women and girls, miserably paid and ready enough to strike at a moment's notice, but notoriously difficult to retain in unions. Time and again the Aberdeen Trades Council, together with visiting organisers such as Lady Dilke, tried to promote trade unionism amongst the textile workers, but the net result was disappointing. A first attempt was made in 1882, and two years later, when two women delegates were accredited to the Trades Council, a local Workwomen's Protective and Benefit Society—later broadened into a Workmen and Workwomen's Society—was in

---

[1] The reason may have been of a political nature: as will be seen later, the ironmoulders disaffiliated for a short period on political grounds.

existence.[1] The society made little headway with recruitment, an influx of new members on the occasion of each strike being quickly followed by a falling-off of membership; and in 1889 it was reported to the Trades Council that Miss Cummings had been dismissed from the Broadford factory 'simply and solely because she was Secretary of the Union', and that other members at Broadford 'were told that they must either leave the Society or leave the Works'.[2] Within a few years, the society was superseded by a branch of the Scottish Mill and Factory Operatives' Federal Union, and this branch was still in existence—and recruiting members— at the turn of the century.[3] Rather more successful, though in a more limited field, was a Carpet-weavers' Society established in 1888 amongst the men at Gordons Mills.

Attempts to establish strong and stable union organisation amongst the paper-workers, one of whose main grievances was long hours of work—in 1889 they were asking for a sixty-eight hour week—were no more successful than amongst the textile workers. Partly, no doubt, this was due to the relative isolation of the paper-workers from the mainstream of events in Aberdeen; partly, it was due to the determination of the employers to prevent the establishment of unions in their mills. The first signs of trade unionism appeared in 1889, when a dispute over wages developed into a lock-out at the Stoneywood mill; in spite of financial help from the Trades Council, the men soon returned to work on the employers' terms, which included a signed statement from the workers to the effect that they would have nothing to do with trade unionism. Three years later, a branch of the Paper Makers' Union was formed at Woodside, but seems to have met with little success: in 1896, the Trades Council was once more deciding to 'try and organise the paper workers'.[4] It is probably more than a mere

[1] *Minutes*, 5 Oct. 1882; 30 Oct. 1884.
[2] *Ibid.* 12 July 1889; 17 July 1889. The Trades Council decided to make up Miss Cummings' wages for a period of two months.
[3] *Ibid.* 7 Oct. 1891; 14 Dec. 1893; 19 Apr. 1899. The branch had a membership of 116 in 1894 (*Daily Free Press*, 19 Jan. 1894).
[4] *Minutes*, 30 Oct. 1889; 4 Dec. 1889; 3 Feb. 1892; 1 June 1896.

coincidence that the Aberdeen branch of the Social Democratic Federation gained its first electoral success when, in
1895, W. Cooper was elected to the Town Council to
represent the outlying ward of Woodside, where textile
and paper workers were strongly concentrated: if these
workers were unable to form stable unions, at least they
knew how to vote.

Trade unionism was also relatively weak and fluctuating
in the fishing industry, where share-fishermen predominated
on the production side and women, working in small units,
on the processing side; and amongst seamen and farm-
workers. In the case of the two latter groups of workers, the
difficulties of organisation, arising from the scattered nature
of the work, are so obvious as to require no elaboration.
The organisations of labourers in the various industries will
be referred to later.

Apart from the granite, building, and shipbuilding
industries, the strength of trade unionism in Aberdeen lay
mainly in the more miscellaneous crafts, especially in the
printing, baking, shoemaking, and tailoring trades. It was
natural enough that there should be fairly strong branches
of the Scottish Typographical Association,[1] the Bookbinders
and Machine Rulers' Consolidated Union, and the Amalgamated Society of Lithographic Printers: Aberdeen's
cultural position in the north of Scotland, together with the
proximity of the paper-making industry, aided the growth
of publishing ventures, and by 1892 there were three daily
and two evening newspapers published in the city.

There was a surprising number of relatively large baking
establishments in Aberdeen, each employing perhaps thirty
or forty men, and this, together with an active policy by the
local leaders of the journeymen bakers, contributed to the
city becoming 'one of the strongholds of trade unionism
among the bakers of Scotland'; in 1888, Aberdeen was
chosen as the first headquarters of the newly-formed Operative Bakers' National Federal Union of Scotland, and A.
Catto, an Aberdeen man, was elected as the first secretary

[1] The existing local Association affiliated to the S.T.A. in 1885.

of the organisation.[1] Almost equally energetic was the local branch of the National Union of Boot and Shoe Operatives; whilst the branches of the Scottish National Operative Tailors' Society and of the Amalgamated Society of Tailors had between them more than 300 members in 1894.

The 'eighties and 'nineties were years when machinery was being adopted, nationally and locally, in the shoe-making and, to a lesser extent, in the baking and clothing trades. In Aberdeen, this growth of factory conditions of production had its reflection in the decline of the old union of hand-bootmakers and the concurrent expansion of the boot and shoe operatives' union; the latter union exerted its efforts in the direction not of retarding the introduction of machinery but of endeavouring to ensure that adequate piece-work prices were fixed for work done on the new machines. On the other hand, the Aberdeen tailors seem to have spent nearly all their energy in comparatively fruitless attempts to prevent the police-clothing contract for the city from going to 'sweating' firms in the south.[2] Of the broader aspects of the growth in the use of machinery and of large-scale production in these and other industries, it may be remarked that it had not progressed so far as to render it virtually impossible for a craftsman to set up in business on his own, though the tendency was in that direction. It was not uncommon for a mason to emigrate to America, accumulate a little capital there, and return to Aberdeen to establish himself in a small way. G. Bisset, blacksmith, and W. Livingston, printer, who were presidents of the Aberdeen Trades Council in 1886-8 and 1889 respectively, both subsequently became employers.

[1] W. Diack, *History of the Trades Council and the Trade Union Movement in Aberdeen* (Aberdeen, 1939), p. 163.
[2] See, e.g., references in *Minutes*, 15 Mar. 1893 (bakers); 13 Mar. 1895 (shoemakers); 5 Jan. 1893 (tailors).

3*

CHAPTER IV

EXPANSION OF TRADE UNIONISM

THE general view of trade unionism in Aberdeen given in the previous chapter conveys no real impression of the dramatic changes in its importance, composition, and outlook in the twenty-two years under consideration. Fortunately, ample material for the reconstruction of the story of these changes exists in the minutes of the Aberdeen United Trades Council—to give it its full title—from the year 1878. These minutes, especially those compiled by W. Johnston, who was the extremely efficient and painstaking secretary of the Council from 1887 to 1907, are a fascinating mine of information.

The Trades Council was formed in 1868[1] and, like similar bodies in other towns, consisted of delegates from affiliated unions or branches of unions. Its constitution provided that one delegate might be accredited for 25 members or less, two delegates for 26 to 50 members, three for 51 to 75 members, four for 76 to 100 members, and one further delegate for each additional 100 members; affiliation fees were to be paid in a similar proportion. Naturally, some unions, notably the masons in the 'nineties, were much more strongly represented than others, but by that time the number of affiliated bodies was so large that no one union

---

[1] On the initiative of the Associated Joiners, in the first instance to organise support for the Aberdeen masons who were then engaged in a strike against a wage-reduction (W. Diack, *op. cit.* pp. 8-10, 133). In a similar way, a Delegated Committee of Sympathy had come into existence in 1846: the Union of House Carpenters and Joiners of Aberdeen was involved in a strike and lock-out (their employers had 'resolved not to treat with any Union, or third party, in a matter which lay entirely between the Workmen individually and their Employers'—statement by employers, *Aberdeen Journal*, 1 April 1846), and the masons' union organised support for them. However, this Delegated Committee—an embryonic Trades Council, whose secretary was Adam Duncan, a Chartist—seems to have been dissolved after about three years.

or allied group of unions exercised dominance in the Council by sheer weight of numbers. There was no block voting, and until 1892 there was a rule that not more than one member of each trade might be elected to the executive committee; in that year the rule was discarded, without any ill effects on the internal democracy of the Council, as being impractical.

The co-ordinating position of the Trades Council and the fact that affiliated societies sent their leading members as delegates, made of it the focus and rallying point of the trade union and Labour movement of the city in the two decades. This was especially recognised at times of crisis: more than one union affiliated during or immediately after a strike in which it was engaged. Through the Council information was exchanged, sectional differences were smoothed out, support extended, and industrial and political campaigns organised and co-ordinated.

In 1878-9, however, the Trades Council and the trade union movement in general were at a very low ebb. In Britain as a whole, trade unions in the 'eighties comprised at the most only about one-fifteenth of the total working population,[1] and there is no reason to suppose that the position in Aberdeen was very different. There were not many trade unions in the city, they catered solely for skilled craftsmen, and their membership was low. The Trades Council was not even representative of this limited number of workers, being made up largely of delegates from shipbuilding craftsmen. Trade unionists were well aware of their weakness in face of depression: when a boilermakers' delegate asked the opinion of the Trades Council as to whether his organisation should resist a reduction of wages, 'the unanimous recommendation was . . . submission until trade should take a change for the better'.[2]

The 'extreme and complicated sectionalism' character-istic of trade unionism at this time[3] was well in evidence in

[1] J. H. Clapham, *Economic History of Modern Britain*, vol. II (1932), p. 154.
[2] *Minutes*, 6 Nov. 1878.
[3] S. and B. Webb, *History of Trade Unionism* (1902), p. 359.

Aberdeen. There were frequent demarcation disputes, accentuated by the prevailing depression but arising essentially out of technical change. The shipwrights, for example, originally worked as carpenters in the building of wooden ships: with the revolution in shipbuilding involved in the substitution of iron for wood, they felt compelled to take up ironworking and so encroached on the sphere of work claimed by the boilermakers and iron-shipbuilders. The boilermakers protested, but the representative of the shipwrights replied that 'in consideration of the depressed state of trade that body could not see their way to interfere so as to stop their members from doing what they could to earn a livelihood'.[1] The Trades Council played a fairly useful part by acting as mediator in a dreary succession of demarcation disputes, but the settlements it was able to effect were usually only temporary in character.[2]

The depression of 1878-9 weakened all unions, and caused the collapse of some of the smaller ones. The rope-makers, for instance, withdrew their delegate from the Trades Council, 'their society being almost broken up'.[3] It is quite clear that the Trades Council itself was concerned only to weather the storm. W. Johnston, a member of the Council at this time, referred in later years to the fact that 'in the days of the monthly meetings, one member sometimes took a nap during the proceedings, a thing that was hardly to be wondered at in view of the nature of the subjects that were discussed . . . one subject discussed was the Channel Tunnel'.[4] Johnston might have added that the date of one meeting was altered, partly because 'it might be inconvenient for some of the members to

[1] *Minutes*, 5 Nov. 1879. Thirteen years later the carpenters and joiners were complaining that the shipwrights were 'infringing upon their trade': evidently the latter body of workers was being driven from pillar to post (20 June 1892).

[2] On the other hand, the statement (S. and B. Webb, *op. cit.* p. 355) that the efforts of Trades Councils to settle such disputes 'almost invariably' ended in the secession of one or other of the contending unions is certainly not applicable to Aberdeen.

[3] *Minutes*, 9 Oct. 1878.

[4] *Daily Free Press*, 6 June 1892. Johnston was in a reminiscent mood.

meet on Wednesday owing to the horse racing occurring on that day'.[1]

From about 1883-4, however, the activity and importance of the Trades Council increased considerably, and its composition and outlook began to undergo important changes, corresponding to changes amongst affiliated bodies. The first signs of the new awakening came in 1882, when the Council held a meeting to which unaffiliated trades were invited. As a result, the number of societies represented at the Council was doubled,[2] and the Council could claim to be representative of the organised craftsmen. In the following year, it was decided to hold meetings fortnightly instead of monthly; and the Council's financial position was very firmly established by the great success of an industrial and art exhibition organised by it, a profit of more than £250 being realised.[3] By 1884, when newspaper reporters were being admitted to meetings and the Trades Union Congress held its annual meeting, by invitation, in Aberdeen, the Trades Council was sure of itself. The bodies then represented at it included the ironmoulders, engineers, boilermakers, blacksmiths, associated joiners, masons, carvers and gilders, cabinetmakers, upholsterers, printers, bookbinders, lithographic printers, tailors, boot and shoe riveters and finishers, bakers, brushmakers, tinplate workers, holders-up, and (factory) workwomen; the shipwrights and the shore labourers were probably also affiliated,[4] together with two or three other unspecified bodies; whilst outside the Trades Council were still several trades such as the amalgamated joiners, plumbers, and brassfounders. The Trades Council represented perhaps 2,000 workers.[5]

---

[1] *Minutes*, 5 Sep. 1881.   [2] *Daily Free Press*, 24 Dec. 1888.

[3] *Minutes*, 1 Feb. 1883. Four more exhibitions were held in the next seventeen years, though none was quite so profitable as the first one.

[4] In the absence of annual reports of the Trades Council, information as to which unions were affiliated in any particular year is derived solely from incidental references to them in the *Minutes*. E.g. the shipwrights' delegates figured in the *Minutes* on 18 Sep. 1883 and 14 Jan. 1885: in the intervening year, there was no reference to them, but this was probably because they did not sponsor any reported resolution of the Council.

[5] It was estimated that the expenses of the forthcoming T.U.C. meeting

It will be noticed that this list of organisations includes a few of semi-skilled or unskilled workers—the line of demarcation is extremely difficult to draw. The Work-women's Protective and Benefit Society has already been referred to; and very little is known of the shadowy Society of Holders-up (boilermakers' helpers). The shore labourers (dockers) struck for higher wages in 1883, and received advice and financial support from the Trades Council. The strike was successful and a local Shore Labourers' Society was then formed, which soon affiliated to the Trades Council.[1] Within a few years, several more organisations of semi-skilled or unskilled workers were formed: a Gas Stokers' Society, which broke up soon after its president had been dismissed from work and the Trades Council had 'thought it advisable not to visit the Gas Works being afraid that their visit there would lead to more of the stokers being dismissed';[2] a Seamen and Firemen's Society, which also lasted only two or three years;[3] a branch of the Scottish Amalgamated Society of Railway Servants;[4] and the Scottish Farm Servants' Union. The formation in 1886 in Aberdeen-shire of this latter body was a remarkable achievement: besides the obvious difficulties inherent in forming a union of farm-workers anywhere, arising from their isolation from one another and from the centres of trade unionism, there

in Aberdeen would be £100, 'about an average of 1s. per head to the con-stituencies of the council' (*Minutes*, 30 Jan. 1884). On the other hand, the Aberdeen Trades Council was listed in the report of the seventeenth annual T.U.C. (1884) as having 4,000 members.

[1] *Minutes*, 20 June 1883; 4 July 1883; 15 Aug. 1883.

[2] *Ibid.* 30 Oct. 1884; 10 Dec. 1884; 30 Sep. 1885.

[3] The Trades Council had grave doubts as to the *bona fides* of the leaders of this body. The rules of the society provided specifically that its secretary and treasurer were *not* to be connected with the profession of seaman or fireman, and one of these officials, J. Martin, was accredited as delegate to the Trades Council. Martin was also secretary of the Aberdeen Conservative Working Man's Association, a fact which did not help to make him *persona grata* to the Trades Council. After considerable hesitation, the Council finally accepted Martin as a delegate, but the society itself disintegrated soon after (*Daily Free Press*, 12 Feb. 1885; *Minutes*, 17 June 1884; 14 Jan. 1885; 26 Feb. 1885; 5 Aug. 1885).

[4] 23 Nov. 1887; 8 Aug. 1888.

was the peculiar difficulty in Scotland that farm servants were engaged for six-monthly or annual periods at hiring-fairs, which not only made concerted action extremely difficult, but made for periodic re-forming—or breaking up —of union branches. Nevertheless, the union was formed, with the help of the Aberdeen Trades Council, though the initiative came from the farm-workers themselves; their main immediate aims were the securing of monthly payment of wages with engagements for indefinite periods, a weekly half-day holiday, and the abolition of the bothy system. These objects were not gained, but in the circumstances the union did well to remain in fairly active existence for a number of years; in 1895 it amalgamated with the Scottish Ploughmen's Federal Union, a more powerful body based on the southern and midland areas of Scotland.[1]

It is apparent from the foregoing account that 'new' unionism, one of the distinguishing features of which was the movement to extend trade unionism beyond the ranks of the skilled craftsmen, had its origins in Aberdeen in the mid-'eighties and cannot be ascribed solely or mainly to the impact of the London dock and gasworks events of 1888-9. One of the most remarkable features of the whole period from the early 'eighties was the way in which the skilled workers represented in the Trades Council did their utmost to encourage less fortunate and less experienced workers to form their own organisations. The growing recognition of the essential identity of interests of the wage-earning classes, and of the narrowing of the social gap between the unskilled workers on the one hand and the skilled workers with their narrow, craft, traditions on the other hand, was in marked contrast to the exclusive attitude, characterised and accentuated by demarcation disputes, of the craftsmen of the previous decade. Not that sectional interests had completely obliterated a more generous and far-sighted outlook even

---

[1] G. Evans, *Trade Unionism and the Wage Level in Aberdeen between 1870 and 1920* (unpublished thesis, University Library, Aberdeen). There were earlier, abortive, attempts to form unions of farm-workers in Aberdeenshire in 1872 and 1881.

in the black days of depression of 1878-9: even then, there had been those who were disgusted with demarcation disputes since they 'believed nothing gave employers so much satisfaction as to see dissensions exhibited among workingmen'.[1] Nevertheless, the change of attitude on the part of the skilled workers in Aberdeen in the 'eighties was very considerable, and suggests that many of the national leaders of the craft unions, their views dominated by a concept of aristocracy of labour, were out of touch with the movement of opinion amongst the humbler members of their unions.

Symptomatic, both of the deep-rooted character of the older view and of the growth of the newer, were the words of J. C. Thompson, president of the Trades Council, in introducing a deputation from the shore labourers, then on strike. He 'trusted that the members [of the Trades Council] would forget that they were masons, joiners, and so many different sections of tradesmen, but that they would keep in mind that they were all workmen and therefore had an interest in the general cause of labour, and in whatever tended to the advancement and elevation of the workman'.[2] The tradesmen responded suitably on that occasion by voting £5 in support of the shore labourers. That the newer view had not yet won a complete victory was shown two months later when the Council, by a narrow majority, decided not to protest at the decision of the Aberdeen Harbour Board that labourers employed by it were not to be paid more than 4d. per hour: most members of the Council took the view that there was no occasion to protest since there was no direct evidence to show that the labourers themselves were dissatisfied or had made any complaint against the Board.[3] No doubt, also, the fact that the boilermakers employed and paid their own labourers did not predispose these craftsmen to look with favour upon labourers: on one occasion the boilermakers were criticised in the local press for paying exceptionally low wages to their labourers, but they were able to satisfy the Trades Council

---

[1] *Minutes*, 19 May 1880.   [2] *Ibid.* 20 June 1883.
[3] *Ibid.* 29 Aug. 1883.

that this was not so and that their conduct had been 'considerate and gentlemanly'.[1] Soon, however, the Trades Council was resolving to 'try to induce those trades that have no union at present to take active steps to form one',[2] and in 1890 it committed itself so far as to decide unanimously 'that it be an instruction of the Council to delegates representing trades in which unskilled labour is utilised to use whatever means they have in their power to get the labourers connected with some labourers' union'.[3] Nor were these empty words.

The position of J. C. Thompson in the movement is of particular interest, since he seems to have acted as a general organiser. Thompson was an ironmoulder by trade, and a delegate to the Trades Council from his union branch. A leading Radical, he was president of the Trades Council from 1883 to 1885, and although he established himself as a newsagent and bookseller some time later, he continued to represent the ironmoulders' union at the Trades Council. Presumably his work as newsagent left him with more spare time than most trade unionists had and, after helping to organise women workers, he became the first general secretary of the Scottish Farm Servants' Union. By 1888, he was also secretary of the Shore Labourers' Society; three years later he was still secretary of the Shore Labourers' Society, and had added to this the position of secretary of the newly-formed branch of the Amalgamated Union of Seamen and Firemen, whilst still representing the ironmoulders at the Trades Council. Such extraordinary activity as this was exceptional, but there were many other men who, with more limited opportunities than Thompson's, devoted all their time and energies to trade union work.

The breaking down of the traditional social barriers between skilled, semi-skilled, and unskilled workers, while it represented 'a widening of the mental horizon, a genuine elevation of the Trade Union Movement',[4] was by no means a matter simply of altruistic sentiment on the part of the

---

[1] *Minutes*, 26 Oct. 1886.
[3] *Ibid.* 28 May 1890.
[2] *Ibid.* 1 Oct. 1884.
[4] S. and B. Webb, *op. cit.* p. 421.

craftsmen. There certainly was an element of this: delegates from the shore labourers' and the gas stokers' societies were elected to the executive committee of the Trades Council in 1885, although neither of these delegates seems to have taken very much part in the deliberations of the Council. Yet, quite apart from sentiment, there were sound practical reasons for attempts to extend the bounds of trade union organisation. The members of the Trades Council who, in the summer of 1886, 'made week-end pilgrimages to the country districts, organised meetings, and proclaimed to the rural workers the message of trade unionism'[1] were well aware of the depressing effect on their own living conditions of the existence of a mass of low-paid workers. In 1891, J. C. Thompson made a renewed appeal to the Trades Council for assistance in organising the farm servants, pointing out that whenever there was a dispute at the harbour in Aberdeen, or on the railways, the blacklegs were drawn from country districts.[2] W. Johnston drew attention to the wider implications when, in an annual report, he referred to the results of a recent census:

'Some of the parishes in and around Aberdeenshire had been depopulated to the extent of some hundreds in a single parish within ten years. The people had found their way to the large centres of industry, and the labour market had, in consequence, become so congested that the labouring classes had barely been able to gain a mere subsistence. The present landed system was rotten to the core, and if some means could be devised whereby an organised effort could be put forth to persuade the people in the rural districts to form themselves into trade organisations for the purpose of securing better terms for their labour, a benefit would be conferred both on themselves and the working classes in the large centres of population.'[3]

An instructive illustration of the growing realisation by craftsmen of the benefits to be derived from 'all grades' organisation concerns the engineers in Aberdeen.   On their

---

[1] W. Diack, op. cit., p. 183.   [2] Daily Free Press, 28 May 1891.
[3] Ibid. 22 Dec. 1892.

own initiative, engineering apprentices at one establishment in 1888 struck work in protest at having to work
fifty-seven hours per week instead of the recognised
fifty-four in the engineering trade, and a deputation was
sent to the Trades Council to ask for support. The local
branch of the Amalgamated Society of Engineers suddenly
woke up to the fact that it was quite out of touch with this
body of potential cheap labour: the union's delegate, after
plaintively referring to the fact that there were so many
apprentices employed 'and not a journeyman in the place',
and expressing the opinion that the apprentices should have
approached the A.S.E. about the matter, took the deputation of apprentices with him to a meeting of the union. The
strike spread, and the A.S.E. took up the apprentices' case,
giving financial support and advice. It was probably this
incident which accounted for the existence, some time later,
of a Society of Apprentice Engineers.[1]

The indications of a new spirit amongst trade unionists
in Aberdeen in the mid-'eighties are important in view of
what was to follow, but it should not be supposed that there
was any very substantial progress made in organisation in
these years. The movement felt the effects of depression: by
the end of 1886 a number of societies had declined in
membership; and the seamen's and gas-stokers' societies
collapsed. Nevertheless, there was no catastrophic general
decline as there had been in 1878-9. In some directions, as
for example with the farm-workers, real progress was made,
and with the coming of better economic conditions in 1888-9
the position of trade unionism in the city was transformed.

One important step was the revival of the masons'
organisation. For a number of years there had been an
Aberdeen lodge of the Scottish Operative Masons' Society,
but the Society was crippled during the depression of the
late 'seventies and never recovered its old position. The
Aberdeen lodge, never strong, dissolved itself in 1886 or
1887.[2] Within two years the masons 'had found since the

---

[1] *Minutes*, 26 Sep. 1888; 18 Oct. 1888; 31 Oct. 1888; 30 Aug. 1892.
[2] R. W. Postgate, *The Builders' History* (1924), pp. 326-9.

old society had become defunct, that there was no rule to regulate the trade',[1] and formed the Aberdeen Operative Masons' and Stonecutters' Society. This, though a local union, very soon became the most powerful trade union organisation in Aberdeen: by the mid-'nineties it had a membership of nearly 2,000, virtually 100 per cent. of those eligible to join, and in 1895 it appointed its first full-time secretary. There was nothing mysterious about this remarkable advance: it was due mainly to the relations established between the masons and their employers. Until 1887, the employers were consistently hostile to any form of trade unionism, but in that year granite manufacturers and quarry-owners united to form the Aberdeen Granite Association, a powerful and far-sighted body. When the masons' union was formed a year later a remarkable agreement was concluded between the two organisations: members of the employers' body were to employ only members of the union, while members of the union were to work only for members of the Granite Association.[2] It is not surprising, then, that the masons' union grew so rapidly. What is rather surprising is that the union did not become very conservative in its outlook in the 'nineties.

Important as was the formation of the masons' union, it was not to be expected that such a body of skilled craftsmen would have long remained unorganised. Quite unexpected, on the other hand, was the eruption, with explosive force, of the 'new' unionism of the early 'nineties. In January 1889 the Trades Council set up a committee 'for the purpose of arranging the better organisation of the working classes in

[1] *Minutes*, 22 Aug. 1888.

[2] The agreement is still (1955) in force, though the masons now form part of the Amalgamated Union of Building Trade Workers. The rules of the Aberdeen Granite Association stipulated that members should charge non-members an extra 25 per cent., and that local granite was to be used as much as possible; while the objects of the Aberdeen Master Masons' Association, as expressed in the revised constitution of 1898, specifically included the maintaining and regulation of prices and price lists (G. Evans, *op. cit.* Appendix C, IV and V: Rules of the Aberdeen Granite Association and of the Aberdeen Master Masons' Association). The monopolistic intentions of the associations are apparent.

Membership Certificate, The Amalgamated Society of Millsawyers
and Woodcutting Machinists, Aberdeen
(Established 1866)

the city and district';[1] and this organising committee
became a standing body of the Council, re-elected annually.
The committee drew up a list of the various groups of
workers who had no union, and decided to begin its work
with the seamen. A meeting of seamen was arranged, the
Shore Labourers' Society offered the use of its hall, and the
Trades Council made itself responsible for the expenses;
J. Havelock Wilson, secretary of the National Amalgamated
Union of Seamen and Firemen, attended at the invitation
of the Council, and a branch of the union was successfully
launched, more than 100 men joining immediately.[2] This
first success of the organising committee set the pattern for
many such meetings in the following years: the Trades
Council, through its organising committee, deliberately
set out to organise a particular group of workers, calling
a meeting of them, bearing the initial expenses, and nursing
the new body until it could stand on its own feet or proved
incapable of enlisting adequate support from the workers
concerned.

Skilled workers were also affected by the new development. A few months after the seamen's meeting, a branch of
the plasterers' union was formed in a similar manner;[3] and
meanwhile, the joiners' and tailors' societies were holding
mass recruiting meetings, with considerable success.[4] Indeed,
the steady, often rapid, expansion of many of the craft
unions in the 'nineties was noteworthy. Naturally, some of
the craft organisations, such as those of the compositors and
shipwrights, were already very well established and showed
little change in size, but most recruited many new members.
For example, the bakers' union branch grew from 120
members in 1887 to 229 six years later; and in the same
period the membership of the branches of the two joiners'
societies increased from 287 to about 430, and by 1900 the

[1] *Minutes*, 23 Jan. 1889.
[2] *Ibid.* 13 Feb. 1889; 6 Mar. 1889. The branch was weakened very soon
after this, when it was involved in a national, and unsuccessful, strike of
seamen.
[3] *Ibid.* 13 Mar. 1889; 8 May 1889; 27 Nov. 1889.
[4] *Ibid.* 22 Mar. 1889; 17 April 1889.

4

joiners had recruited several hundred more members, so that there was not a single non-unionist carpenter or joiner in Aberdeen.[1] Here, again, the Trades Council's organising committee played its part.

But it was rather the spectacular progress made in forming new unions, notably of the unskilled, which attracted —rightly—most attention in the 'nineties. As the Webbs put it: 'Within a year after the dockers' victory probably over 200,000 workers had been added to the Trade Union ranks, recruited from sections of the labour world formerly abandoned as incapable of organisation.'[2] Enough has been said to indicate that a movement of this character would probably have occurred in Aberdeen in these favourable years without the impetus given by the London dock strike in late 1889. Nevertheless, the effect of that strike should not be underestimated: the tidings came to those in Aberdeen who were already working on similar lines as a sign and an inspiration that they were not working alone, and that the apparently helpless and hopeless mass of labourers could be organised. Nor was Aberdeen quite so isolated from the national movement as its geographical position might lead one to suppose: in 1891 alone, H. H. Champion, Keir Hardie, Ben Tillett, and Tom Mann all addressed meetings there on different occasions. Typical of the character of such meetings was the motion carried at the conclusion of that addressed by Mann under the auspices of the Trades Council: ' That this meeting recognises the deep necessity for an extension of trade and labour organisations, and especially urges upon labourers of all grades to at once organise, in their own interest as well as that of their fellows. '[3]

Leaving political development aside for the present, some indication of the strength of the new movement in Aberdeen may be derived from the fact that in three years, 1890-2, unions were formed by painters, tinplate workers, fishermen, cabmen, coachbuilders, brushmakers, papermakers, upholsterers, and builders' labourers, and probably

[1] Daily Free Press, 27 Dec. 1887; 19 Jan. 1894; 2 Mar. 1900.
[2] S. and B. Webb, op. cit. p. 406.   [3] Daily Free Press, 11 April 1891.

also by coopers, horse-shoers, and rope and twine spinners and hemp dressers. Some of these new bodies, for example, the painters, paper-workers, and upholsterers, were branches of national unions, others were local societies; some were formed in order to conduct strikes, others were formed as a result of successful strikes. Real progress was not so striking as might be inferred from this long list: some of the new unions, particularly the local ones such as the cabmen and horse-shoers, broke up within a few years; while others, such as the coachbuilders, brushmakers, and upholsterers— mainly craft unions—had had a fleeting existence in Aberdeen at varying times in the 'eighties, and were now re-formed on a more permanent footing. Repeated endeavours to recruit more women workers met with little success, and a fresh attempt to organise the gasworkers, made this time by Pete Curran, national organiser of the Gasworkers' and General Labourers' Union, again ended in failure in face of the hostility of the management.[1]

Nevertheless, with these qualifications, there was a very substantial expansion of trade unionism in Aberdeen in these years. It was reflected in the strength of the Trades Council. W. Johnston, the secretary, reported in December 1890 that whereas there had been only twelve affiliated societies in 1882, and twenty-four in 1884, the number had increased in every year since then, until there were thirty-three affiliated societies, sending a total of over 130 delegates to the Trades Council; one month later, the number of trade unionists represented by organisations affiliated to the Trades Council was 6,951, a figure which Johnston believed was one-half of the total number of working-men in the city. J. Keir, president of the Council in 1894, brought out the change graphically when he remarked, referring to a photograph of the executive committee of twenty-five members, that 'a little more than a dozen years ago the members of the Council did not number all told the number who were in this group'.[2]

---

[1] *Minutes,* 15 April 1891; 20 April 1891; 22 April 1891; 28 April 1891.
[2] *Daily Free Press,* 25 Dec. 1890; 5 Feb. 1891; *Minutes,* 4 July 1894.

More than a mere change in numbers was expressed in this expansion. There was a hardening of the aggressive spirit, in industrial as in political matters, which had begun to be apparent in the late 'eighties: economic conditions were favourable for obtaining concessions from employers, and workers did not waste the opportunity. An extreme instance of this aggressive attitude, exemplified in a refusal to tolerate bad conditions, relates to the girls employed at the Belmont Laundry. In sudden protest at having to work very long hours, these unorganised girls went on strike. The Trades Council endeavoured to negotiate on their behalf, but was informed by a deputation from the girls that they were determined not to go back to the laundry on any terms; they preferred to find work elsewhere—and they found it.[1] Militant action was seen as a means of advancing trade unionism: a delegate from the stone polishers' union referred to the satisfactory conclusion of a 'slight dispute' with the employers, and 'mentioned it had done the society good as they had augmented their number by 50 additional members';[2] proposals were made and accepted at the Trades Council for drawing up blacklists of non-union shops and firms in various industries, the intention being to promote a boycott of such establishments.[3]

The growth of solidarity, of fraternal feeling between various sections of the working-classes, was very marked on a local scale but extended also to the national, and even international, sphere. There was very considerable discussion in the Trades Council on the question of a general federation of trades.[4] Since the national aspects of this

[1] *Minutes*, 3 Aug. 1892; 5 Aug. 1892; 24 Aug. 1892.
[2] *Ibid.* 16 April 1890. The stonepolishers' union, a local body, was formed in 1888. Its rules provided for a subscription of 3d. per week per member; union funds were to be used exclusively in payment of strike allowance, for cases in dispute or arbitration, and management expenses. In 1894, however, a sick benefit scheme was introduced (*Daily Free Press*, 26 Oct. 1888; 25 Dec. 1894).
[3] *Minutes*, 15 Oct. 1890; 22 Oct. 1890; 29 Oct. 1890. Some doubt was expressed as to the legality of such a procedure.
[4] E.g. see *Minutes*, 13 Nov. 1889; 22 Jan. 1890; 9 April 1890; 22 April 1890; 31 Jan. 1891.

proposal were under consideration by the T.U.C., discussion in Aberdeen eventually concentrated on the possibility of forming a local federation of trade unions: it was hoped that such a federation, based on the Trades Council but more organically knit together than that body, would be able to rid the movement of demarcation disputes, facilitate the securing of permanent premises in Aberdeen, lay the basis for better-organised political work,[1] and be a more satisfactory way, by means of levies, of providing for inter-union support during trade disputes.

It was this last point which was probably the most important consideration. The whole discussion arose naturally out of the local and national conditions of repeated strikes at the time and of the changed outlook of trade unionism : the immediate local impulse came from the fact that when the question first came before the Trades Council, in November 1889, that body had out amongst its affiliated unions subscription sheets soliciting financial support for the Forfar mill-workers on strike, the Dundee hammermen also on strike, and the rights of crofters against encroaching lairds on the hill of Bennachie in Aberdeenshire—and a few weeks later, money was being raised on behalf of locked-out paper-workers at the Stoneywood mill. It is not surprising, therefore, that trade unionists should be seeking a more regular means of providing financial support for unions involved in disputes. Not that the Aberdeen Trades Council was ever slow to extend financial and moral support when its sympathies were aroused. It had, in fact, a remarkable record for generosity in this respect in the late 'eighties and the 'nineties. Ignoring the numerous local disputes, one may single out the following instances of donations by the Council: £1 to the Bristol Trades Council towards the expenses of defending a number of bakers charged with conspiracy and intimidation;[2] £5 for the Australian general

[1] The proposal under discussion envisaged a levy of ½d. per week for each member of affiliated bodies, which would yield 'something like £600, and with a sum like that they could send a man to Parliament, and perhaps two or three men to the Town Council' (T. Nicol, president of the Trades Council, reported in *Daily Free Press*, 13 Nov. 1890). [2] *Minutes*, 19 Mar. 1890.

4 *

strike;[1] £32 for the Scottish railwaymen's strike;[2] £5 for the Durham miners;[3] £11 for the Scottish miners;[4] unspecified sums for strikers in St. Petersburg and Hamburg;[5] and over £4 for the Danish general lock-out.[6] Such assistance was not indiscriminate: on one occasion, the Trades Council refused to support a local strike by non-union engineers, on the ground that these men had 'a good union of their own they could have joined'.[7]

Proposals for a general local federation of unions proved too ambitious at the time, but the discussion was not fruitless. One important outcome was the purchase by the Trades Council of property and the building of a hall and offices to serve as a permanent centre;[8] at the same time, W. Johnston was appointed full-time secretary of the Council,[9] and affiliation fees were increased. The Council had become a permanent institution.

It is very difficult to estimate precisely the part played by unskilled and semi-skilled workers in Aberdeen in the expansion of the early 'nineties. Apart from a small local society of builders' labourers, formed in 1892, labourers were catered for mainly by the Aberdeen branch of the Scottish Farm Servants' Union—so much so, indeed, that the union was sometimes referred to in the Trades Council minutes as the Scottish Farm Servants, Carters, and General Labourers' Union.[10] The carters composed the core of the branch, and

[1] *Minutes*, 2 Oct. 1890.   [2] *Ibid.* 8 July 1891.
[3] *Ibid.* 25 May 1892; 6 July 1892.
[4] *Ibid.* 1 Aug. 1894; 29 Aug. 1894; 19 Sep. 1894.
[5] *Ibid.* 29 July 1896; 9 Dec. 1896; 16 Dec. 1896.
[6] *Ibid.* 27 Sep. 1899. Some of these donations were made directly out of Trades Council funds; others were raised amongst trade unionists, on appeal by the Council.
[7] *Ibid.* 12 Feb. 1890. On the other hand, the Council usually gave financial support to non-union women workers in a dispute (*Minutes*, 15 Mar. 1899).
[8] *Ibid.* 21 Jan. 1891; 22 Feb. 1892; 4 Dec. 1895; 6 May 1896. At least £3,500 was borrowed to cover the cost of the buildings, the first of their kind owned by any Trades Council in Britain.
[9] At a salary of £15 a year, with £1 per week, rent free, as caretaker of the new premises (*Minutes*, 11 May 1892; 31 Aug. 1892).
[10] E.g. *Minutes*, 27 May 1891.

the association with farm-workers was natural: very many general labourers in the city had worked on the land and retained links with the countryside, whilst the carters, to put the connection no higher, worked with horses. The branch was fairly active, but no figures of its membership at the time are available; it was probably fairly strong among the carters, and very weak among other groups of general labourers. It produced two or three sturdy and reliable leaders from its own ranks, such as Proctor and Angus, but its most prominent representative was W. C. Mitchell, a clerk who had joined the union for want of a more appropriate organisation.

Besides this union, there was the local Amalgamated Society of Combmakers, an organisation formed in 1889; a weak branch of the railway servants' society; and the organisations of the seamen and the shore labourers. In 1891 the seamen's union struck work in opposition to the attempt of the British Shipping Federation (of which there was a branch in Aberdeen) to induce unionist seamen to work with non-unionists. The union was defeated, and along with it the Aberdeen Shore Labourers' Society, whose members had come out in sympathy with the seamen. It then became apparent that the employers involved had more far-reaching aims: 'it was quite evident all the Federation wanted was to smash the union', by refusing to employ unionists.[1] And, indeed, by the end of 1893 no organisation of either seamen or dockers existed in Aberdeen; an attempt in that year to form a branch of the London dockers' union, to replace the defunct local society, ended in failure.[2] These

---

[1] *Minutes*, 18 Feb. 1891; 4 Mar. 1891; 18 Mar. 1891. This struggle occurred at a time when the Aberdeen seamen's branch was weakened and in bad odour as a consequence of a demarcation dispute between fishermen (members of the seamen's union) and the Tyne Steam Packet Society, a union which had some members in Aberdeen. J. C. Thompson, the seamen's secretary, was severely criticised by trade unionists for having attempted to squeeze out the members of the Tyne society (*Minutes*, 7 June 1890; 18 June 1890; 31 Jan. 1891; 25 Mar. 1891).

[2] *Ibid.* 21 June 1893; 27 Dec. 1893; *Aberdeen Labour Elector*, 25 Feb. 1893. A number of wood-sawyers who had joined this short-lived branch of the London dockers' union then formed a local sawmillers' and machinists' union.

were serious losses to trade unionism locally: the seamen's union branch had had more than 600 members in 1890.

The reaction of employers to the new unionism of the early 'nineties was not uniform. At the first impact, many employers were clearly very much worried. Some of the more far-sighted realised at once that trade unionism must now be recognised as a permanent feature of social life, and that the problem was to devise adequate forms of machinery for negotiating with it and containing it. Probably the best illustration of this attitude on the part of some employers is the agreement, already referred to, between the Aberdeen Granite Association and the masons' union, strengthening the position of both bodies. And if the granite merchants were very quick off the mark, the general body of employers, with some exceptions, were not slow to follow. On 26 December 1889, within a few months of the London dock strike, the Aberdeen Chamber of Commerce resolved that in view of the prevalence of labour disputes and strikes it was desirable that efforts should be made by chambers of commerce throughout the country towards the establishment of boards of arbitration and conciliation. A motion to this effect, proposed by the Aberdeen Chamber, was adopted at the annual meeting of the Associated Chambers of Commerce of the United Kingdom in March 1890. The Aberdeen Chamber of Commerce then made an indirect approach to the Trades Council, the latter body responded, and by the end of the year the Aberdeen Conciliation Board had been established, consisting of five representatives each of employers and workers, with an independent chairman— together with a number of subordinate trade conciliation committees.[1] In the following decade the Board, meeting in

---

[1] *Minutes*, 19 Mar. 1890; 16 Apr. 1890; 3 Sep. 1890; 2 Oct. 1890; *Aberdeen Conciliation Board* (pamphlet, Aberdeen, 1891). The Trades Council favoured the scheme, though some delegates had their doubts about certain members of the Chamber of Commerce. The Marxists of the Aberdeen Socialist Society said that the Conciliation Board and its work reminded them of the rhyme:

'There was a young lady of Riga
Went out for a ride on a tigah;
They came back from the ride with the lady inside,
And a smile on the face of the tigah.'

(*The Workers' Herald*, 9 Jan. 1892).

the offices of the Chamber of Commerce, had some limited successes in settling industrial disputes, but its powers were limited: where it attempted to conciliate parties to a dispute, its conclusions were recommendations only, and it could act as an arbitration board only when expressly requested to do so by both parties.[1] Nevertheless, partly as a result of the Board's work, there was a noticeable elaboration of local codes of by-laws defining conditions of work between employers' and workers' organisations in a number of industries, particularly the various branches of building.

On the other hand, many employers, especially after the first impact of new unionism had worn off, resorted to more old-fashioned methods of dealing with unions: refusal of recognition or negotiation, victimisation, and attempts to break unions. In addition to the successful offensive by dockland employers, the following examples of this attitude may be cited: the manager of the municipal gasworks refused to meet a deputation of workers;[2] the combworkers complained of 'petty tyranny', of letters being ignored, and of victimisation of members of the union;[3] and the boot and shoe operatives, after a strike, alleged that 'if a man left his employment he was unable to get a job in the three surrounding counties on account of the combination of the employers'.[4] Such methods were naturally better adapted to, and more commonly employed in, dealing with relatively weak groups of workers such as seamen, carters, and paper and textile employees than with the traditionally highly organised artisans.

In the depression from 1892 to 1895, there was the usual decline in trade union membership in Aberdeen. The

[1] In the joiners' strike of 1893-4, the employers refused the workers' request to call in the Conciliation Board as arbiter, and this gave rise to an interesting debate in the Trades Council concerning the unsatisfactory status of arbitration boards. Eventually, the Council affirmed its blunt opposition to any form of compulsory arbitration, and rejected, by thirty votes to nineteen, a compromise amendment favouring legislation to put arbitration boards on a better footing by giving them power to summon parties in dispute to submit their cases, but no power legally to enforce the decisions of such boards (*Minutes*, 28 Feb. 1894; 14 Mar. 1894).   [2] *Minutes*, 22 April 1891.
[3] *Ibid.* 16 Oct. 1890; 14 Oct. 1891.   [4] *Ibid.* 3 Sep. 1890.

seamen's and dockers' organisations collapsed, and so did the granite polishers'; and a number of other unions were in 'a somewhat languishing position'.[1] The Trades Council represented only 4,679 workers in January 1894: a decline of more than 30 per cent. in three years, though this was partly due to disaffiliation by a number of societies, such as the boilermakers', engineers', and railway servants'.[2] Yet this decline was not reflected to any marked extent in the activity of the Trades Council and many of its constituent bodies. Naturally, this was particularly so in the case of workers in the building industry, relatively unaffected by depression: painters, plasterers, sett-makers, and joiners succeeded in obtaining wage-increases in 1893;[3] and in the following year, the joiners defeated a determined attempt to reduce their wages, while the sawmillers' union secured a reduction of working hours from fifty-six to fifty-four without any loss in wages.[4] But it was not only the builders' unions which remained active. The Trades Council did much fine work in collecting and distributing relief for the unemployed, and its organising committee continued its attempts to encourage unionism amongst unorganised workers. Successes in this direction were much less marked than formerly, but in 1894-5 there made an appearance a local plasterers' labourers' society, and branches of the National Amalgamated Coal Porters' Union, the National Union of Insurance Agents, and the Amalgamated Musicians' Union—the two last-named organisations being the first specifically designed for black-coated workers in the city.

The response of the trade union movement to the lifting of the general economic depression was very rapid, and in

[1] *Minutes*, 24 Feb. 1896. The granite polishers' union was revived later in 1896.

[2] *Daily Free Press*, 19 Jan. 1894. See Appendix, Table IV. The figure of 4,679 may not be a true indication of the position, as credentials of societies were often not sent in until February in each year. The three societies named re-affiliated in 1895.

[3] *Aberdeen Labour Elector*, 11 Mar. 1893; 1 April 1893; *Minutes*, 8 Nov. 1893.

[4] *Ibid.* 11 April 1894.

the last few years of the century the general advance was resumed. One big failure was registered in the collapse of the farm-workers' union. In 1895, the Scottish Farm Servants' Union amalgamated with another to the south to form the Scottish Ploughmen and General Labourers' Union; but the amalgamation did not succeed in preventing a decline, and by 1900 no farm-workers' organisation remained in Aberdeenshire. With this exception, however, the forward movement of trade unionism in Aberdeen in the years from 1896 to 1900 was comparable in many ways with that of the late 'eighties and early 'nineties. Indeed, in some respects the later movement might be considered the more important of the two. To the earlier movement must be assigned the credit for having made the first substantial attempt to bring unskilled workers into the trade union fold, but the organising campaigns of that period were hasty and improvised; experience was lacking, and little thought was devoted to the problems of the specific form of organisation required to meet particular circumstances. As has been shown, a number of the bodies then formed were ephemeral. Moreover, it seems that the movement to organise unskilled workers was less successful at the time in Scotland than in England and Wales: in 1892 in the two latter countries there were, out of a total of 1,324,000 trade unionists, 302,880 labourers and transport workers, while the comparable figures in Scotland were 147,000 and 21,670.[1]

By contrast, the development of the late 'nineties in Aberdeen represented a less spectacular but more permanent and satisfying growth; ground temporarily lost was recovered and consolidated, roots struck deeper, and significant changes in forms of organisation took place, based on the experience of the earlier expansion. W. Johnston summed up one lesson that had been learned when he gave his annual report to the Trades Council for the year 1900: 'Local societies have never been a success. Employers can and do find means of knowing what is in the exchequer and

---

[1] Estimated by S. and B. Webb, *op. cit.* p. 428.

calculate to a nicety how long the funds will last.'[1] And indeed there had been important moves in the direction of forming stronger and wider trade union groupings. One expression of this was the formation, in 1895, of the Aberdeen Building Trades Federation, an alliance of all the building workers' organisations—joiners, painters, plasterers, slaters, plumbers, sawmillers, quarrymen, and builders' labourers —with the exception of the masons. The bodies comprising the federation retained their independence of one another, but aimed at presenting a united front in support of the agreed demands of any section within the industry. In conjunction with the Trades Council's organising committee, the federation was then instrumental in bringing into existence a branch of the Scottish National Labourers' Union; this was designed mainly to replace the two existing local societies of builders' labourers and plasterers' labourers, which had not met with much success.[2]

Similarly in a wider field, when Trades Councils were excluded from the British T.U.C. by the coup of 1895, the Council in Aberdeen felt its isolation keenly, and lost no time in attempting to fill the gap: it convened a conference of representatives of Trades Councils in Scotland to consider the position.[3] This conference, held in Dundee on 9 November 1895, confined itself mainly to recording a protest against the arbitrary action of the Parliamentary Committee of the T.U.C., and to appealing to trade unions for support: it was hoped that the decision to exclude Trades Councils might yet be reversed.[4] A few months later, however, when it had become apparent that there was little likelihood of this being done, the Falkirk Trades Council took the initiative in convening a further conference, which met at Falkirk

[1] *Daily Free Press*, 27 Dec. 1900. But there was one successful local union, that of the masons.
[2] *Minutes*, 3 Mar. 1896; 8 April 1896. It is a striking commentary on the conditions of trade union work amongst labourers, and on the poverty of such workers, that some trade unionists in Aberdeen considered that the 3d. per week membership contribution of the National Labourers' Union would preclude a number of workers from joining.
[3] *Ibid.* 11 Sep. 1895; 16 Oct. 1895.
[4] *Ibid.* 7 Nov. 1895; 4 Dec. 1895; *Daily Free Press*, 11 Nov. 1895.

on 25 April 1896 and was attended by all the more important Scottish Trades Councils, together with the Stirlingshire miners' organisation. The conference approved the principle of a Scottish federation of trade unions, 'in view of the numerous federations of employers' organisations',[1] and set up a committee to formulate draft proposals. The committee's proposals were accepted in Edinburgh on 11 September, and in March 1897 the first annual meeting of the Scottish T.U.C. took place, one delegate from the Aberdeen Trades Council being amongst the approximately sixty present.[2]

As already noted, the late 'nineties were years of rapid expansion of trade unionism in Aberdeen. In the early phases of this movement, something of the temper of the early 'nineties was seen: there were considerably more trade disputes in Aberdeenshire in 1896 than in any year since before 1888. This time the emphasis was more markedly, and more successfully, upon organising unskilled workers. The city branch of the Scottish Ploughmen and General Labourers' Union began to recruit carters rapidly,[3] and applied for a wage-increase for them. The Aberdeen Master Carters' Association, however, refused to recognise the union and, in 1897, 700 carters came out on strike, the issue of union recognition looming as large in their eyes as that of the requested wage-increase. For the first time in Aberdeen, a strike of unskilled workers was successful; the carters gained a wage-increase, and the union, now recognised, benefited accordingly.[4] By the end of the year, the union was strong enough to establish a second branch in the city,

---

[1] *Daily Free Press*, 27 April 1896. It should be remembered that the movement towards combination amongst the workers in the 'eighties and 'nineties was paralleled by a similar movement amongst employers. For example, in Aberdeen the existing separate masters' associations of joiners, masons, plumbers, painters, plasterers, and slaters united to form the Aberdeen branch of the Master Builders' Federation in 1899.

[2] *Minutes*, 20 May 1896; 23 Sep. 1896; 19 May 1897; *Daily Free Press*, 26 Mar. 1897.

[3] *Minutes*, 26 Aug. 1896.

[4] *Ibid.* 14 July 1897; 28 July 1897; 11 Aug. 1897. Carters' wages were raised from 20s.-22s. per week to 22s.-25s.

the distinction between the two branches being one of occupation not of geography: one branch catered for general labourers, the other for carters. Soon after, a third branch was formed, this time for ironworkers' labourers.[1] Meanwhile, in 1897, a branch of the Liverpool dockers' union was formed, along with branches of the tenters' (Dundee textile) union, the Iron Dressers' and Brass Dressers' Union, and the National Amalgamated Union of Shop Assistants, Warehousemen, and Clerks.[2] J. Keir, president of the Trades Council, thought that probably in no previous year during the Council's existence had there been so great an increase in the number of trade unionists as in 1897;[3] and a year later, W. Johnston reported that 'the membership showed an increase over any previous year. One very pleasant feature was that this increase was from what is known as unskilled workmen. Never in the history of the Council had so much progress been made in this connection. The dock labourers had a membership of 700, and other classes of labourers were also benefiting to a considerable extent.'[4]

Fresh ground was opened up amongst transport workers when a branch of the Scottish Hackney-Carriage and Tramway Employees' Union was formed, with an initial membership of 140, in 1899; and at the same time, the Gasworkers' and General Labourers' Union at last succeeded in establishing a branch among the gasworkers of the city.[5] Having gained a foothold, this powerful union soon extended its influence. For some time it had been apparent that, with the exception of the three branches in Aberdeen, the Scottish Ploughmen and General Labourers' Union was disintegrating. Dissolution came in 1900, and coincided with a strike by Aberdeen carters in which, through lack

---

[1] *Minutes*, 13 July 1898. This new development arose from a strike of labourers at a big foundry.

[2] *Ibid.* 2 Dec. 1896; 11 Aug. 1897; 16 Dec. 1897. The branch of the shop assistants' union soon broke up, and was re-formed in 1900 (*Minutes*, 3 Oct. 1900).

[3] *Daily Free Press*, 30 Dec. 1897.   [4] *Ibid.* 29 Dec. 1898.

[5] *Minutes*, 17 May 1899; 4 Oct. 1899; 25 July 1900.

of funds, they failed to repeat their success of three years earlier. All three branches—carters, general labourers, and ironworkers' labourers—then joined the Gasworkers and General Labourers' Union, 'which would be more effective if any dispute arose than a local union'.[1] A further illustration of the desire for greater unity between associated groups of trade unionists was the formation by carters, ironworkers' labourers, and dock labourers of a local federation of labourers.[2]

The labourers' organisations were beginning to feel their feet, beginning to assert themselves not only against employers but also against groups of craftsmen unwilling to treat them on terms of equality. One of the first actions of the federation of labourers was to ask the advice of the executive committee of the Trades Council as to how to proceed 'in reference to the question of tradesmen taking labourers' work'.[3] The ironworking labourers had already had occasion to complain that whilst they were on strike craftsmen had taken over their work: in reply, the secretary of the local branch of the ironmoulders' union, while stating his willingness to do anything reasonable to forward the interests of the labourers, had put forward the significant explanation that 'in a moulding shop it was a difficult matter to define what was really moulding work and what was labourers' '.[4] Evidently, the dividing line between craftsman and labourer, at least in this particular branch of industry, had a considerable element of artificiality about it.

Yet another organisation formed at this time was that of the trawl fishermen. An attempt was made to form a seamen's union again,[5] but was apparently unsuccessful. However, in 1899 the Aberdeen Steam Fishing Vessels Enginemen and Firemen's Union was formed, and it quickly established itself as a stable body: within a few

---

[1] *Minutes*, 5 Sep. 1900. For the carters' strike, see *Daily Free Press*, 3 April 1900; 13 April 1900.   [2] *Minutes*, 6 Sep. 1899.
[3] *Ibid*. 6 Dec. 1899. The advice profferred was that the federation should, in the first instance, approach the unions whose members they complained of.
[4] *Ibid*. 30 Nov. 1898; 14 Dec. 1898.   [5] *Ibid*. 4 Nov. 1896.

months it had enrolled more than 400 members.[1] It was not an organisation of unskilled workers, since it deliberately excluded from membership deck-hands and cooks.

By 1900, then, the trade union movement in Aberdeen had reached a peak, best expressed in the status of the Trades Council which had contributed so much to it. The small and relatively unimportant Council of the late 'seventies had grown and changed almost beyond recognition. It was more representative than ever before: only one or two unions remained unconnected with it, and even the plumbers, who had long preferred isolation from the local movement, had at last affiliated to the Council. And it was larger than ever before: by the end of 1900, forty-six trade union bodies were affiliated, with a local membership of more than 8,000.[2]

[1] *Minutes*, 13 Dec. 1899; *Daily Free Press*, 9 May 1900. In addition, the Tyne Steam Packet Society had 200 members in Aberdeen.

[2] *Ibid.* 28 Dec. 1899; 27 Dec. 1900; *Minutes*, 27 Dec. 1899; 24 Jan. 1900.

PART III
ANALYSIS

CHAPTER V

WAGES, TECHNICAL CHANGE, AND INTENSITY OF LABOUR

It is a familiar enough story that trade unionism has usually expanded, both in numbers and activity, in the prosperous years of the upswing of the trade cycle, and conversely has contracted in periods of depression. The movement in Aberdeen was certainly no exception to this general rule, and the correlation is clear. But why should there have been such an abnormal expansion of trade unionism in the city in the late 'eighties and the 'nineties? Why did it find its political expression in a marked swing away from Liberalism towards the concept of an independent Labour party? No clear-cut or complete answer to such questions can be given on the basis of available material, but an examination of some of the economic and social factors involved—leaving political matters aside for later discussion—does provide some clues.[1]

The years from 1878 to 1900 fall almost wholly within the period of the Great Depression and should, in the first place, be viewed against the background of that peculiar phase of British economic and social development: a background of expanding production, yet of relative technical stagnation, falling prices, and declining rates of profit; of the first real questionings of the value of free trade, a heightened interest in empire and sheltered markets, a quickening movement towards combination amongst employers; of a revival of Socialism, paralleling the great expansion of trade unionism. Restlessness amongst workers had its counterpart in the unease, persistent gloom, and loss of confidence amongst employers and politicians as, with

[1] See the discussion of these problems in E. J. Hobsbawm, 'Economic Fluctuations and Some Social Movements since 1800' (*Econ. Hist. Rev.*, 2nd ser., vol. V, no. 1, 1952, pp. 1-52.)

cut-throat competition, the rate of profit fell, social tension mounted, and the relative technical progressiveness of Germany and the U.S.A. began to be apparent. A middle-class social conscience grew up alongside economic in-dividualism: social investigators like Booth uncovered the teeming mass of poverty and degradation amongst labourers in London and other towns; Toynbee set to work, and others came to be 'squires' of East London. Heaving misery demanded the attention of Victorian society and could no longer be ignored.

It is now accepted that real wages rose considerably during the Great Depression from 1873 to 1896, mainly through the mechanism of falling prices. But the precise timing of the movements of wages, which may have in-fluenced the attitudes of workers, is not so clear. The available national indices of wages, cost of living, and unemployment are admittedly unsatisfactory and artificial,[1] but those for the crucial period of the 'seventies and 'eighties, for what they are worth, seem to indicate that money-wages fell from their boom peak in 1873-4 by rather less than 10 per cent. in 1880, and then remained more or less stationary until about 1888; that real wages for workers who remained in full employment showed a continuous rise throughout the 'seventies and 'eighties; and that average real wages, allowing for unemployment, fell somewhat between 1873 and 1880, then rose considerably until 1883, and were still at that level three years later:[2] this latter calculation is, of course, a peculiarly artificial one and is virtually useless. Inconclusive evidence of the consumption of certain staple goodss suggest that real wages may have fallen in the years 1886 to 1889.[3]

Available evidence of wages in Aberdeen, though incomplete, is rather more satisfactory than these inadequate national figures. The level of wages in the city was influenced

---

[1] Cf. E. J. Hobsbawm, *loc. cit.* pp. 3-4.

[2] W. Rostow, *op. cit.* p. 90; A. L. Bowley, *Wages and Income since 1860* (1937), pp. 30, 34, 122-3.

[3] E. J. Hobsbawm, *loc. cit.* pp. 9-11.

by a number of related factors: the trade cycle, and national wage-movements; the state of the labour-market; and the strength and attitude of trade unions. The importance of the trade cycle in making it relatively more easy or difficult for employers to grant increases or impose reductions of wages is obvious, though it needs to be studied in relation to the position of trade unions. Wages of workers in Aberdeen were always lower than those of comparable workers in other British towns, and they tended to follow national wage-movements: in the 'nineties, for example, the joiners, whose wage-rates were regularly 1d. or 1½d. per hour below those of joiners in Glasgow and Edinburgh, usually secured an increase shortly after—perhaps a year after—such increase had been secured by their fellow-unionists in the other two cities.[1] The state of the labour-market is a more complex problem, and comparatively little statistical information on it is available, varying as it did from one industry to another. The position was complicated by the fact that Aberdeen was not only the centre of a very wide agricultural area in the north-east of Scotland, but that that area had an abnormally high rate of emigration. In the spring of each year, considerable numbers of farm-workers, domestic servants, and craftsmen (especially masons) went overseas to South Africa, Australia and New Zealand, the U.S.A., or Canada. In part, the flow was seasonal, masons in particular often returning from America in the autumn of the same year: a glutted labour-market for monumental masons in 1894 was made worse by depression in the American granite industry, the comparatively few Aberdeen masons who emigrated in the spring returning in the autumn of that year, together with many others who had gone to the U.S.A. in previous years.[2] The exceptionally high rate of emigration[3] from the north-east undoubtedly had an effect on the labour-market locally, particularly in the 'eighties,

[1] *Daily Free Press*, 16 Mar. 1900; 19 Mar. 1900; 20 Mar. 1900. Dundee joiners' rates were usually ½d. per hour above those of Aberdeen.

[2] *Ibid.* 25 Dec. 1894.

[3] The Aberdeen Trades Council lost two presidents, Elphinstone in 1882 and Robertson in 1900, in this way. They were both masons.

5 *

by partially offsetting the growth of the city through migration to it from the countryside. The short-lived rise in farm-workers' wages in the north-east about the year 1884 —a rise which had no parallel in other parts of Britain—was probably due, at least in part, to the particularly high rate of emigration from the area at the time.[1] One outstanding example of the dimensions which the movement of emigration could assume may be cited here: in 1899-1900, when the building boom had ended, emigration of unemployed building masons developed, and according to the *Daily Free Press*, 'whereas there were between 1,100 and 1,300 masons engaged in Aberdeen last year, there are only some 600 to 700 in Aberdeen now'.[2]

Emigration reacted on a labour-market which was normally fluid. The mobility of workers in the city was very high and in almost every considerable strike or lock-out there was a movement out of the city, to the south or overseas, by many of the men involved, in search of work, often only temporarily. Employers, for their part, could usually obtain general labour from the neighbouring agricultural districts, in cases of industrial disputes and in more normal times, but found it much more difficult to secure skilled workers from outside to replace craftsmen on strike: apart from the implications of blacklegging and the pressure exercised by strike-pickets, Aberdeen was relatively isolated geographically and wages were lower than in any town to the south. Consequently, a strike of craftsmen was broken by such means only in times of severe national depression, as in 1878 when the joiners were beaten by an influx of men from the west of Scotland. Yet although such peculiarities of the situation, especially that of emigration, had their importance, and tended to keep wages higher in the 'eighties than they might otherwise have been, their importance should not be over-estimated. A high rate of emigration was

---

[1] R. Molland and G. Evans, *loc. cit.* pp. 225-6. Similarly, farm wages offered at spring hiring-fairs, when labour was in greater demand, tended to be higher than at the autumn fairs.

[2] *Daily Free Press*, 15 Nov. 1900. The figures do no tinclude monumental masons.

a feature of the 'eighties, but not of the 'nineties;[1] and it was in the latter decade that the population of Aberdeen, and its labour-force, increased the more rapidly. But it was precisely in the 'nineties, despite the fall in emigration, that the greater improvements in wages and other conditions were obtained by workers: the difference was due largely to the increased strength and activity of the trade unions.

Fairly reliable indices of wages in Aberdeen are available for seven groups of workers: from 1870 for monumental masons, building masons, carpenters and joiners, bakers, and farm servants, and from 1877 for first-class scavengers employed by the Aberdeen Corporation Cleansing Department, and seamen and firemen.[2] Before these indices may be used, however, some explanation of their limitations must be given. They are indices of wage-*rates*, not of earnings; they relate only to time-rates of payment, not piece-rates; the figures for farm servants are not strictly comparable, since these workers often received, over and above their known cash wages, perquisites of varying value, such as accommodation and food; and the wages of the first-class scavengers should not be taken as truly indicative of those of general labourers—for example, second-class scavengers' rates were usually from 2s. to 5s. below those of the first-class men in the 'seventies and 'eighties.[3]

Moreover, the wage-rates referred to must be treated with extreme caution, since in most cases they were rates recognised by the union concerned, but not necessarily actually paid to all workers. The bakers' weekly wage-rate, for example, was described as a minimum, but in 1893,

---

[1] 'For the six years 1893-9 it [net emigration] had sunk very low indeed. For the whole of the then United Kingdom it had averaged only 53,000 a year; had never risen above 76,000; and in one year (1894) was under 38,000. Deducting the Irish—however many they may have been—this leaves only an inconsiderable figure for Britain' (J. H. Clapham, *op. cit.* vol. III, p. 40).

[2] See Appendix, Table V, taken from G. Evans, *op. cit.*

[3] On the other hand, some shore labourers could, in exceptional circumstances, *earn* as much as 32s. per week, though this included much night-work and was not an average (*Minutes*, 20 June 1883).

when the 'minimum' was 21s., there were said to be bakers
in the employment of the Northern Co-operative Company
'toiling from Monday morning till Saturday night for 14
shillings a week'.[1] In the case of the masons and joiners—and
building craftsmen generally—the wage-rate is that of the
'standard': by the early 'nineties it had become an established
custom that this standard rate should be paid to not less
than three-quarters of the men in each firm, while the
remaining one-quarter might be paid less.[2] The probability
is that the later the date and the stronger the union—the
two tended to coincide, with the development of local
agreements between workers and employers—the more did
both 'minimum' and 'standard' approximate to the actual
rate paid to the greater number of workers: in 1893, out of
about 500 journeymen building masons in Aberdeen, 130
were paid above, and only about 20 below, the standard;
out of about 800 monumental masons, 400 were paid over
the standard, and about 100 below it; while of the joiners
and carpenters, less strongly organised than the masons,
perhaps more than one-quarter received less than the
standard—in some cases, 1d. per hour less.[3]

Nevertheless, with all their limitations, the wage-indices
of the seven groups of workers do indicate fairly clearly the
general trend of wages in Aberdeen. The pattern which
emerges is one of rising money-wages in the early and mid-
'seventies, followed by a sharp fall towards the end of the
decade; wages then remained virtually stationary in the
'eighties, but rose about 1890, and again from about 1896
—by which latter date prices had begun a general upward
movement. For example, the building masons, the most
highly paid of the groups, received a standard rate equivalent to nearly 30s. a week in 1870: increases brought this
up to more than 31s. by 1877, but in the following two years
it fell to a little over 27s. The rate remained at this level
until 1890, when it rose to 29s.; further increases in 1896 and

---

[1] *Minutes*, 15 Mar. 1893.
[2] *Aberdeen Labour Elector*, 18 Mar. 1893; 25 Mar. 1893.
[3] *Ibid.* 15 April 1893; 22 April 1893.

1898 brought it up to over 33s.[1] Thus there had been a rise of 5 per cent. 1870-6, a fall of 13 per cent. 1878-9, and a rise of 23 per cent. 1890-8.

The general trend was much the same for the other groups of workers—except the seamen and firemen—though with some variations: the carpenters and joiners, with a rate equivalent to over 25s. in 1870, received abnormally large increases in the next six years, and these were not fully cancelled out by 1880 when the rate was 27s.; farm servants' wages in 1880-1 were also still above those of 1870, and between 1881 and 1884 there was a short-lived rise which was more than cancelled out by 1888; the bakers' 'minimum', starting from a low level of 19s. in 1870, rose to 21s. in 1877, and remained unchanged at that figure until 1896-1900, when four successive increases brought it up to 28s. The wages of Aberdeen seamen and firemen employed in the coasting trade[2] fluctuated considerably, and it is not easy to discern any particular trend in them except that they were noticeably higher in the few years when the men's union was active, as in 1884 and at the turn of the 'eighties.

It is unfortunate that only one index of wage-rates of labourers is available, that of the first-class scavengers employed by the Aberdeen Corporation, from 1877. These men then worked for a rate of 19s.; they continued to receive this rate for the next twelve years, but increases in 1889 and 1896 brought it up first to 19s. 6d. and then to 22s.[3] A few isolated figures of wages may be of some slight use: in 1883 labourers employed by the Aberdeen Harbour

[1] Masons (and carpenters and joiners) were paid on an hourly basis, at fortnightly intervals. The weekly rates given have been computed on the basis of an average week of fifty-five hours 1870-1, and fifty hours from 1872. The difference in hours accounts for the fact that, for example, on a *weekly* basis the masons received less in 1879 than in 1870, whereas on an *hourly* basis (as shown in Appendix, Table V) they received as much in the latter year as in the former.

[2] In the coasting trade, wages were paid weekly. Men employed in long sea voyages were paid rather less, and on a monthly basis. It is to be assumed that, in contrast to other workers, no overtime payment could be earned by seamen.

[3] They were paid on a weekly basis (for a sixty-two-hour week until 1889 when it was reduced to fifty-seven hours).

Board were paid a maximum of 4d. per hour, and in 1885 the Board was taking on unemployed men as labourers for 3d. and even 2½d. per hour;[1] wages of tramway workers in 1893 ranged from 21s. to 24s. per week;[2] at the end of the century cabdrivers were receiving wages of 18s. or 19s. per week, described by the president of the Trades Council as 'starvation wages'.[3] On the other hand, the minimum wage recognised by the plumbers in 1900 was 34s.,[4] a surprisingly high rate which may help to explain, in part, the relative aloofness of the plumbers' union from the Trades Council in the previous decade or two.

It should not be supposed that the wage-movements of the seven selected groups of workers necessarily reflect accurately those of all workers; some discrepancy is apparent, for example, in the shipbuilding industry, which was exceptionally sensitive to the trade cycle. Shipbuilding wages fluctuated violently: heavy cuts in 1878-9 were at least partially restored in the following few years; there were further reductions in 1885, yet the *Daily Free Press* 'understood' that in spite of this, shipbuilding wages were still some 10 to 15 per cent. higher than the slump level of 1879—but they were cut again in 1886.[5] Such fluctuations were probably important in themselves as influencing the attitudes of particular groups of workers, but it does not seem likely that they would affect materially the general trend of wages discernible in the comprehensive figures for the seven groups of workers referred to.

Examination of real wages[6] over the whole period shows that the improvement in the standard of living of the workers in Aberdeen was much more marked than the indices of money-wages suggest. Over the years 1870-7,

---

[1] *Minutes*, 29 Aug. 1883; 11 Mar. 1885; *Daily Free Press*, 23 Dec. 1885.
[2] *Aberdeen Labour Elector*, 11 Feb. 1893.
[3] *Minutes*, 10 July 1901. At this time the cabmen went on strike, not only for higher wages but also in an attempt to have the hours of Sunday work reduced to twelve.   [4] *Ibid.* 24 Jan. 1900.
[5] *Daily Free Press*, 30 Dec. 1885; 25 Dec. 1886.
[6] Miss G. Evans (*op. cit.*) considers it legitimate to apply to Aberdeen A. L. Bowley's index of the cost of living in Great Britain for the period.

when fluctuations have been discounted, there was no real change in the cost of living; it fell somewhat after 1877, and then dropped sharply in 1884-6; a slight rise in 1888-91 was followed by a steady fall until 1895-6 when it began a long upward movement. Consequently, there was an increase in the real wages of the seven groups of workers in the 'eighties, despite the fact that money-wages remained virtually unchanged. Indeed, it is clear that by 1886 the sharp fall in money-wages which had occurred in 1878-9 had been more than compensated for by the fall in the cost of living. And, excluding the seamen from consideration, the increase in real wages continued, with some slight setbacks, until about 1897-9. For the period 1878-1900, the building masons and the first-class scavengers may be taken as fairly typical: in both cases, money-wages increased by about 14 to 16 per cent., and real wages by perhaps 35 to 36 per cent., the proportionate increases being slightly greater for the scavengers than for the masons.[1]

By far the greater part of the increase in real wages was secured in the decade from 1889. It was certainly not a coincidence that the same decade witnessed a very rapid increase in trade union strength and activity, but it would be futile to attempt to establish definitively that it was the changed position of the unions which was mainly responsible for the improved conditions of their members. To attempt thus to separate union activity from economic forces favourable for securing better conditions for workers would be artificial.[2] Some examples have been given of trade unionists

[1] The absolute percentages are not important in themselves, since a slight change in the dates chosen makes a considerable difference: e.g. for the period 1877-99, the increase in money-wages would be 13 to 16 per cent., and that in real wages 45 to 48 per cent.

[2] An interesting example of the 'pure' effect on wages of economic conditions, apparently irrespective of trade unionism, concerns the masons. In the 'seventies and 'eighties the building masons received ½d. per hour more than the monumental masons; but in the early 'nineties, when the building industry was in a more prosperous condition than the monumental granite, the differential was increased to 1d. per hour and remained at that figure. Both building and monumental masons were members of the same union though in separate branches of it.

securing higher wages or defeating proposed wage-reductions by strike action. All that can usefully be added is the remark that, in the absence of sliding-scales—which themselves depend upon the existence of an organised body of workers —wage-increases are seldom or never granted automatically, however favourable economic conditions may be. Nor, of course, is the existence of a strongly organised trade union necessarily a guarantee that wage-increases will be obtained when economic conditions are ripe for it: its policy and attitude and leadership must be taken into account. In Aberdeen in the 'nineties there was a large group of able trade union leaders, backed by the members of their branches, who seldom indulged in wildcat strikes—such as there were occurred mainly amongst unorganised workers, for example, in the paper and textile mills—but who were determined to take full advantage of economic conditions favourable for securing better wages and other conditions.[1] Improved conditions and increased trade union strength went hand in hand, the one reacting upon the other.

Interesting as may be the figures of wages in Aberdeen, they are not of very great value in explaining the abnormal trade union expansion of the late 'eighties and early 'nineties. However, one or two significant pointers appear, especially when the figures are submitted to more detailed analysis. For the first time in the memory of very many workers, there was, in the late 'seventies, an appreciable fall in money-wages—a fall which was accompanied by a near-paralysis of trade unionism. The decline in wages was resented by workers, who considered that 'employers were taking rather

[1] It is suggested by E. H. Phelps Brown and P. E. Hart in 'The Share of Wages in National Income' (*Econ. Journal*, vol. LXII, 246, pp. 253-77) that the increased share of wages in the national income at this time was due to the effective use of greater trade union strength in a situation where the 'market environment' precluded employers from maintaining or raising prices proportionately to wages. The market environment in Aberdeen certainly was of that character; year after year employers' complaints of 'keener prices' and 'excessive competition' were heard, and in 1896 it was reported that 'the excessive keenness of competition that goes on has led to a movement among [monumental granite] manufacturers in the city towards a common basis for estimates' (*Daily Free Press*, 26 Dec. 1896).

an undue advantage of the present slackness in trade' by
making extensive and repeated reductions of wages;[1] the
Aberdeen joiners, admitting defeat in a strike, 'considered
it their best policy to give in and take advantage of the first
favourable opportunity for regaining their position'.[2] A
strong impression is conveyed that the shock of the collapse
of these years bit deep into the consciousness of many trade
unionists, who sustained themselves with the grim determination to recover lost ground and to build their organisation anew when times were more propitious.

The peak money-wages of 1877 for masons, carpenters,
and farm servants were not again reached by these groups
of workers until the 'nineties or later. But it was not only
money-wages which were at stake. The years of the 'eighties
are often considered *en bloc* as a period of rising real wages :
in fact, however, the real fall in the cost of living did not
begin until about 1884. In 1884, the real wages of masons
and carpenters, and probably of farm servants, were still
lower than they had been in 1877; though this was not true
of the bakers and scavengers, who had not been subject to
the cyclical wage-reductions of the late 'seventies. Such
evidence of lower real wages is suggestive when it is remembered that 1884 marks the real beginning of the trade union
expansion, both industrial and political, in Aberdeen. And
although the real wages of all groups of workers showed a
consistent upward trend from 1884, the trend was broken
by slight falls for masons, carpenters, and bakers, in 1889-
90 and 1892 : these slight falls may have had an effect on
the events of those years.

Apart from these possible short-term influences of wage-
movements on the timing of the trade union expansion, it
seems not unlikely that the very fluctuation of wages in some
industries, especially shipbuilding in the late 'seventies and

---

[1] *Minutes*, 4 Dec. 1878.

[2] *Ibid.* 6 Nov. 1878. Equally resented was the action of some employers,
in shipbuilding for example, in lengthening working hours, an action condemned by the Trades Council as being 'entirely uncalled for', and which
'ought only to be accepted under the strongest protest' (*Minutes*, 29 Mar.
1879).

early 'eighties, contributed by increasing the restlessness and uncertainty of workers. It cannot have been conducive to the stability of life and peace of mind of the boilermakers in Aberdeen that they should have their wages reduced by 17 per cent. in 1879, have the cut restored or even more than restored in the next few years, only to be faced with further reductions in 1885-6—and at the same time to have to meet the probability of being unemployed for a spell.

Contemporary Aberdeen did not find a Booth or a Rowntree to record a picture of social conditions, but the evidence of wage-rates is alone sufficient to indicate the existence of dire poverty amongst many workers. The piece-work earnings of women textile workers were so low that the Trades Council decided[1] to charge the local branch of the Scottish Mill and Factory Workers' Union only half the usual fees. Working-class housing conditions were appallingly bad, and Leatham was not exaggerating when he remarked that workers in the city 'herded with biggish families in two-roomed tenements that had no bath. One outside closet and water-tap served for six families.'[2] True, the Aberdeen Town Council, at the prompting of independent Labour members, condemned and ordered the closing-down of 177 exceptionally bad slum dwellings in 1893,[3] and overcrowding was being relieved by the building of block after block of tenements, but housing conditions remained bad: the new tenements themselves consisted of one- or two-roomed apartments which usually lacked rudimentary conveniences. Yet such poor social conditions were not fresh elements in the situation in the 'eighties and 'nineties; housing conditions, judged from the standpoint of a later age, had always been bad, just as wages had always been low, hours of work long, and poverty ever present. In all these respects there was an improvement in the period: no useful explanation

[1] *Minutes*, 9 Mar. 1897. The concession was not extended to any other body.
[2] J. Leatham, *loc. cit.* vol. XXVIII, no. 330, p. 13.
[3] See *Aberdeen Labour Elector*, 1 April 1893; 15 April 1893; 22 April 1893; 29 April 1893. One of the owners of this condemned property was the chairman of the Public Health Committee of the Town Council.

of contemporary social movements may be given in terms of any absolute worsening of living conditions. What was new in the situation, by comparison with the years following the decline of Chartism, was not real poverty but 'felt' poverty: workers were acquiring a new stature and dignity, and were not inclined to bear patiently with unsatisfactory conditions or to regard them as the inevitable price of industrialisation.

Of considerable importance in this connection were the social tensions produced by technical change and increasing intensity of labour. Technical change often led to a worsening of conditions for workers: in 1893, a number of tinplate workers at a preserving factory in Aberdeen went on strike in protest at a reduction of piece-work rates which followed the introduction of new machinery; the workers were defeated mainly because the new machinery made possible a considerable supersession of labour.[1] Technical change was not very rapid during the Great Depression but it did affect some industries appreciably at crucial periods; for example, printing, shoemaking, and clothing in the late 'eighties and 'nineties. Amongst such groups of workers the consequent discontent, arising from such factors as displacement and down-grading of labour, was not always expressed in an identical manner: in Aberdeen, the journeymen tailors attempted to stand out against the new machinery and tended to remain Liberal in politics, whilst the boot and shoe operatives tried rather to control piece-work prices for machine-work, and became strong advocates of independent Labour action in politics—as did the printers and bakers.

Similarly, the general though slow trend, through the growth of semi-skilled groups of workers, towards the breaking down of the exclusive and exalted economic position of craftsmen found varying reflections amongst different groups of artisans. The ironmoulders in Aberdeen seem to have envisaged their best interests as lying in the maintenance of an increasingly artificial barrier between themselves and the

[1] *Aberdeen Labour Elector*, 25 Feb. 1893; 4 Mar. 1893; 1 April 1893.

ironworking labourers; the shipwrights, weakened by the technical revolution in shipbuilding, considered themselves 'obliged to be more submissive to their employers than they otherwise would be'[1]—though their submissiveness was not very noticeable in practice, and by the early 'nineties they were no longer Liberal in political outlook. But although there were these divergent reactions by groups of workers to technical change, the general effect was discontent, more usually expressed in increased militancy and a move to the left in politics—a marked contribution to the more co-operative and sympathetic attitude of craftsmen towards labourers. The Rev. A. Webster, Unitarian minister in Aberdeen, knew his audience of working-men when he asserted, in 1887, that 'the hand of labour was withered by unemployment, and by the reckless introduction of machinery which made acquired skill as useless as if the craftsman's hand had been stricken of the palsy'.[2]

Rapid technical change affected only a comparatively small number of industries, but in others expanded production was achieved by speeding up work, by an increased intensity of labour. As a corollary of this, in the 'seventies and 'eighties there was a weakening of restrictive trade union regulations concerning such matters as apprenticeship, piece-work, and overtime.[3] Local evidence relating to such increased pressure on workers—in part a response by employers to falling profit—is fragmentary but suggestive. There are signs of attempts to replace some craftsmen by unskilled cheap labour, thereby exerting pressure on craftsmen to accept work at wages below the standard: Annand, a masons' representative, complained of the systeaticm working of overtime in the stonecutting trade, said to be particularly prevalent in 'the many small yards which had sprung up of late years, and where those employed were chiefly young lads or apprentices', and considered that there

[1] *Minutes*, 19 May 1880.
[2] J. Leatham, *loc. cit.* vol. XXVIII, no. 330, p. 12.
[3] Cf. W. Rostow, *op. cit.* pp. 93-4; E. J. Hobsbawm, *loc. cit.* pp. 13-15, 18-19.

were 'gross infringements' of statutory factory regulations in the employment of these young people; whereupon the Trades Council expressed its conviction that 'the present staff of Factory and Workshop Inspectors is totally inadequate to enforce the due observance of the law as regards the employment of young persons and other conditions specified in the Act of 1878'.[1] There are further indications of a weakening of apprenticeship regulations: the boiler-makers and iron-shipbuilders were involved in a dispute with their employers 'in consequence of the violation of the apprentice law, which stipulates the proportion of apprentices to the number of journeymen employed by the various firms';[2] the engineers apparently had little control over the number of apprentices employed, many of whom, in 1888, were working longer hours than the men; and the printers at one firm came out on strike 'in connection with the apprentice question'.[3]

Evidence of an increased intensity of work and of a tightening of labour discipline, together with resentment by the workers concerned, is more frequently found. In 1885, the president of the Trades Council condemned 'in no measured terms' the proposal of the Jute Company that its workers should operate two looms each; a few months later, these jute-workers were complaining 'with regard to a bonus that had been offered to workers who earned a certain sum of wages per week, their complaint being that when the wages were increased the point at which this bonus became payable was also increased, but when the wages were reduced no reduction was made on the amount entitling the workers to this bonus';[4] and a decade or so later, after a strike against bad conditions at the jute-works, it was alleged 'that the material there was as bad as ever and that

[1] *Minutes*, 30 July 1884. [2] *Ibid.* 13 April 1881.
[3] *Ibid.* 19 Mar. 1890; 2 April 1890. On the other hand, conditions were different in the settmaking trade: there the men themselves employed the apprentices. When the employers wanted a larger number of apprentices taken on in 1900, the settmakers made a counter-claim for an increase in wages to enable them to do this (*Daily Free Press*, 16 Mar. 1900).
[4] *Minutes*, 25 Mar. 1885; 14 Oct. 1885.

6

fines had been severer and more prevalent than formerly'.[1] The Trades Council took up the case of a combmaker who had been dismissed by his employers for refusing to sign a three-year engagement;[2] the gas stokers had a dispute with their employers not only over an increase in pay but also against 'a new system of working introduced' at the gas-works.[3] Anderson, one of the masons' representatives, reported to the Trades Council in approving tone that one master-mason had of his own accord reduced working hours from fifty-one to forty-nine, with no reduction in wages; the Trades Council expressed its satisfaction but another masons' delegate, Rennie, was inclined to be more critical of this particular employer, 'pointing out that it was on account of the great intensity of labour in his work that he had raised the business carried on by him'.[4]

Two further examples, concerning the bakers and the trawl-fishermen, may be given as illustrating the importance attached by workers to the removal of various restrictions associated with a tightening of labour discipline. The journeymen bakers, besides matters affecting wages and their constant demand for the abolition of night-work, were concerned to secure uniformity of hours. The union objected strongly to the fact that some journeymen had to go to work exceptionally early in the morning in order to carry out preparatory work, and in this objection the workers found themselves involved in a constant struggle over a period of years with the Northern Co-operative Company, the largest employer of bakers in the city. The position was complicated for the union by the fact that it had comparatively few members amongst the employees of the company, which tended to be hostile towards trade unionism. The struggle reached its climax in 1897, when the directors of the company proposed that their early bakers should start work at

---

[1] *Minutes*, 31 May 1899.   [2] *Ibid.* 11 Sep. 1889.

[3] *Ibid.* 30 Sep. 1885. It was said that 'sometimes men wrought nine hours all day and then took their turn of night shift thereby working 17 hours out of the 24' at the gas works (*Minutes*, 20 April 1891).

[4] *Ibid.* 5 Aug. 1891.

3 a.m.; at once, the proposal 'considerably accelerated' recruitment to the union of bakers employed by the Co-operative Company; the Trades Council adjourned one of its meetings 'so that as many members as possible could attend the Half-Yearly Meeting of the Northern Co-operative Company to assist in defeating the proposal for the early start by the bakers', and the directors of the Company were compelled to come to terms with the union concerning the starting-hour. Meanwhile, the union had considerably increased its strength, and henceforth the Company dropped its anti-unionist policy.[1]

In a somewhat similar way, the main immediate aim of the Aberdeen Steam Fishing Vessels Enginemen and Fire-men's Union—indeed, one might say the issue on which the Union was formed in 1899—was not to secure higher wages but to break the employers' practice of compulsorily retaining 1d. per day from the workers' wages towards a provident fund controlled by the trawl-owners themselves. The union was not successful in achieving this aim for many years, but it did provide the first foundation on which the union was built.

It is suggested, then, that increased intensity of labour, and the restlessness which it provoked amongst workers, made a considerable contribution to the trade union explosion of the late 'eighties. Such increased intensity seems to have been less marked in the 'nineties: a new and more stable level seems to have been reached, particularly amongst the craftsmen, and in some cases improvements were secured. The granite polishers, for example, 'got some alterations in the working of systematic overtime, and in working during meal times which would benefit them to some extent'.[2] The whole question of persistent overtime was a burning one in the 'eighties, and opposition to it as a system was frequently expressed by engineers, ironmoulders,

---

[1] *Minutes*, 15 April 1891; 10 Oct. 1894; 10 Feb. 1897; 24 Feb. 1897. The other baker-employers in the city usually tended to follow the lead of the Northern Co-operative Company.

[2] *Ibid.* 16 Mar. 1892.

masons, joiners, and other groups of workers in Aberdeen. The question was, however, inseparably connected with that of unemployment—most trade unionists saw no sense in 'working themselves out of a job' or in having some workers on overtime whilst many others were unemployed—and the importance of unemployment was such as to merit separate treatment.

CHAPTER VI

UNEMPLOYMENT AND THE EIGHT-HOUR DAY

ALTHOUGH the fourth quarter of the nineteenth century in Britain was perhaps not marked by significantly higher unemployment than the average from about 1850 to 1914,[1] there was probably more unemployment in 1879 than in any other year during the second half of the century (except 1858), and the mid-'eighties were years of heavy and continuous unemployment.[2] In the chapter on economic fluctuation, stress has been laid upon the fact that Aberdeen escaped relatively lightly from the depression of the mid-'eighties, but there was, nevertheless, considerable unemployment and distress in the city, particularly amongst workers in the shipbuilding and engineering industries. Some examples of this have already been given; in more general terms, the *Daily Free Press* reported that, in shipbuilding, 'misery and want have fallen to the lot of not a few of those who have thus been deprived of their employment, while the great majority have had to accept less remunerative work to keep them from starving'.[3] By the end of 1885, when the depression had deepened, J. C. Thompson was reporting to the Trades Council that its executive committee had the names of 808 unemployed persons and that, in his belief, the real number was over 1,000: even in

---

[1] Much depends upon the periods chosen. W. Rostow, *op. cit.* p. 48, shows that average unemployment was 4·8 per cent. 1855-73, 4·9 per cent. 1874-1900, and 4.5 per cent. 1901-13. D. H. Robertson, *Utility and All That and Other Essays* (1952), pp. 195-6, points out that, on the basis of the same figures, average unemployment was 4·6 per cent. 1851-73, 5·4 per cent. 1874-95, and 4·0 per cent. 1896-1914; he concludes: 'I cannot help thinking there is *some* justification for the impression that for a quarter century, jobs were less secure than they had been or were about to become.'

[2] W. Rostow, *op. cit.* pp. 48-9; J. H. Clapham, *op. cit.* vol. III, p. 6. Unemployment statistics, based on trade union figures, take no account of short-time working, a factor of considerable though unmeasured importance.

[3] *Daily Free Press*, 25 Dec. 1884.

6 *

the granite industry, which had had a 'fairly good' year, some masons were then working a seven-hour day instead of the usual eight hours in the winter months.[1] In the two following years, the *Daily Free Press* was able to sum up the general position in Aberdeen in no more cheerful terms than that 'It is admitted by those who have the best opportunities of gauging this distress that it has assumed at least as great proportions as at the corresponding period last year'; and 'the distress among the working classes of the city is not any keener or more extended than at the corresponding period last year'.[2]

Such unemployment and short-time working vitiates the usefulness of wage-figures. Mackintosh, a boilermakers' representative, admitted that of the 279 members of the Aberdeen branch of the union about 95 might, in good times, earn as much as £3 per week each, although the remainder, on time rates of pay, would average 28s.;[3] but in 1885, when Mackintosh made this statement, trade was not brisk, and it was estimated that in the shipbuilding and allied industries in Aberdeen the number of men employed was only about one-half the number for a good year. Even if full statistical information were available, it would be quite artificial to attempt to construct a graph of the wages of a mythical average worker, with allowance made for average unemployment: the unemployed worker was concerned neither with averages nor with the level of wages of employed workers but with the fact that he was receiving no wages at all for the period of his unemployment.

There was, of course, no State dole, and in Scotland the able-bodied unemployed had no legal right to poor relief. An unemployed worker who had no savings of his own, or who had exhausted them, had few sources of assistance available to him: he might, for a period, receive unemployment benefit from his trade union—but most workers were

---

[1] *Daily Free Press*, 10 Dec. 1885; 30 Dec. 1885.
[2] *Ibid.* 25 Dec. 1886; 27 Dec. 1887.
[3] *Ibid.* 24 Dec. 1885. Mackintosh was replying to local press criticisms that boilermakers did not save money in good times in preparation for bad.

not trade unionists, and many unions in Aberdeen, such as the masons', had no unemployment section of their friendly benefits until the twentieth century; he might belong to a friendly society[1] dispensing unemployment benefit; or he might receive assistance, in cash or kind, from one or more of the charitable organisations, of which the most important in Aberdeen was the Association for Improving the Condition of the Poor. Alternatively, he and his family might starve.

As with poverty, so with unemployment: one of the features of the 'eighties was the way in which workers increasingly 'felt' it, and tended to refuse to accept it as their inevitable lot. The heavy unemployment of 1878-9 was borne almost in silence in Aberdeen: the Trades Council asked the Town Council to provide work for the unemployed, and was dissatisfied with the reply that a large number of persons were being employed in clearing snow from the streets, but took no further action.[2] In the mid-'eighties, however, some development of the working-class attitude towards unemployment was apparent. The Trades Council held a public meeting on the question of relief for the unemployed in 1885, and seems to have instituted a relief fund of its own, though probably not much money came in by way of subscriptions. More significant was a sharpening of attitude towards the Town Council and towards the Association for Improving the Condition of the Poor—a sharpening of attitude indicative both of a growing belief in an absolute right to work and of increasing hostility to charity and the way in which charitable donations were handled. At one Trades Council meeting, 'a great deal of unfavourable comments were made with reference to the dilatoriness of the Town officials in providing immediate work';[3] at another, J. C. Thompson, the president, referred

---

[1] According to W. Johnston, there were not less than twenty lodges of friendly societies in Aberdeen, with a membership of about 9,000, of whom 'about eight thousand would be Trade Unionists, the remaining thousand would be chiefly clerks, shopkeepers, etc.' (*Aberdeen Labour Elector*, 29 June 1893).

[2] *Minutes*, 18 Dec. 1878; 8 Jan. 1879.

[3] *Ibid.* 23 Dec. 1885.

to the number of unemployed, and continued: 'I may say
there is considerable objection among a great many of the
working men to go through the ordeal in connection with
applying to the Association for Improving the Condition of
the Poor. I believe a number of working men would sooner
walk in at a jail door than walk up the steps to that place.'[1]

There was reason for such criticism of the Association:
it was a body which drew voluntary donations from a well-
meaning middle-class public, but its methods were frequently marked by a harsh and unsympathetic attitude
towards the poor. Lord Provost Matthews, speaking at the
sixteenth annual meeting of the Association, referred to the
unemployed in the following terms: 'Some again say that
they will not work for $2\frac{1}{2}$d. an hour, and they will rather
starve than work for less than 4d. Well, I think that these
are the class that should at once be allowed to try the
starvation process before we relieve them.'[2] In the circumstances, it was not surprising that a month later Mackintosh,
the boilermaker, was 'combating warmly the idea of any
surplus [from the relief fund] being handed over to the
Association for relieving the poor'.[3]

There was heavy unemployment again in Aberdeen in
the depression of the early 'nineties. It was apparent in the
winter of 1891-2, when W. Johnston, in his annual report
to the Trades Council, stressed the need for shorter working
hours and for the abolition of systematic overtime and
unrestricted piece-work.[4] In the following winter, estimates
of the number of unemployed in the city varied between
1,000 and 1,500;[5] shipyard workers were particularly
affected, W. Johnston asserting 'that in four of the chief
Unions associated with the Shipbuilding, Shipping, and
Iron Trades over 200 skilled workers were unemployed, and

[1] *Daily Free Press*, 10 Dec. 1885.   [2] *Ibid.* 23 Dec. 1885.
[3] *Minutes*, 3 Feb. 1886. No member of the Trades Council suggested that
a surplus should be disposed of in this manner.
[4] *Daily Free Press*, 24 Dec. 1891. The question of piece-work did not affect
all trades alike: amongst the joiners in Aberdeen it was 'happily all but
unknown' (*Aberdeen Labour Elector*, 18 Mar. 1893).
[5] *Ibid.* 21 Jan. 1893; 4 Feb. 1893.

that each of those necessarily dragged out with him one or more unskilled workers'.[1] There was no marked improvement in 1893-4, although 'one redeeming feature of the present time was the cheap supply of food for the people';[2] and a peak of social distress was reached in the severe winter of 1894-5, when 'unemployed stonecutters filled the street corners'.[3]

The reaction of working-class organisations to this bout of depression followed much the same lines as in the mid-'eighties, but was carried much further and pursued more energetically than before. Once again there was criticism of the Association for Improving the Condition of the Poor: it was attacked by the *Aberdeen Labour Elector* for 'almsgiving' and for not realising the extent of distress in the city; and W. S. Rennie, a masons' delegate and himself unemployed, 'felt rather hurt' at the news that a list of the unemployed, drawn up by the Trades Council and given to the Lord Provost, had been made available to the Association.[4] By this time, a new and active working-class organisation was in existence: the Aberdeen Socialist Society was busy holding meetings of the unemployed, sending deputations to the Town Council to ask for relief works, and engaging in general propagandist work concerning the nature and causes of unemployment.[5] The views of the Society were expressed by some of its members who were also members of the Trades Council. W. Cooper, for example, in putting a successful motion calling upon the Town Council to begin relief works upon a large scale, 'held that charity was no solution to the unemployed [*sic*] difficulty'.[6]

The Trades Council was still the focus of working-class effort in connection with unemployment. It sent a deputation to the town magistrates, but this was not productive of immediate results, and in the winter of 1892-3 the Council

[1] *Aberdeen Labour Elector*, 18 Feb. 1893.
[2] W. Johnston, reported in *Daily Free Press*, 20 Dec. 1894.
[3] *Ibid.* 26 Dec. 1895. There were others besides stonecutters.
[4] *Aberdeen Labour Elector*, 28 Jan. 1893; *Minutes*, 3 Feb. 1892.
[5] See, for example, *The Workers' Herald*, 16 Jan. 1892.
[6] *Minutes*, 15 Feb. 1893.

opened a relief fund of its own and appointed a large committee to administer it in every ward of the city; £175 was
collected by the Trades Council for relief of the unemployed
in that winter.[1] The Town Council, in response to urgings,
itself appointed relief committees—which included representatives of the Trades Council—and opened relief works
in the form of digging for a park and a new gasometer
'somewhat ahead of schedule'.[2] In the following winter the
Town Council again appointed a special relief committee,
but took no action in 1894-5; it was then, when distress was
at its height, that the Trades Council emerged indisputably
as the main agency for the relief of the unemployed in
Aberdeen. The relief fund was re-opened, a register of the
unemployed was kept in the Trades Council offices (in one
week the number of names on it was 1,340) and for months
most of the members of the Council had their evenings
occupied in visiting applicants for relief and distributing
food, clothing, and money to necessitous cases[3]—though
they found time to endorse the action of the president in
sending a telegram to Keir Hardie, 'strongly approving of
his action in the House of Commons for the appointment of
a Committee to consider the question of the unemployed'.[4]
By June 1895, when the relief fund was closed, the Trades
Council had collected £976 5s. 1d., together with goods and
clothing of an estimated value of £600; of the money,
£824 3s. 2½d. had been distributed in relief.[5]

A good example of the importance which the problem
of unemployment assumed in the eyes of the Trades Council
at this time may be derived from the interest which that
body showed in the Parish Council. There was little opportunity for working-class participation in the activities of the

[1] *Minutes*, 4 Feb. 1892; 1 Feb. 1893; *Daily Free Press*, 21 Dec. 1893.
[2] *Minutes*, 15 Feb. 1893; J. Leatham, *loc. cit.* vol. XXIX, no. 343, p. 12.
[3] W. Diack gives a vivid picture of this work, *op. cit.* pp. 49-55. See also
Minutes, 23 Jan. 1895; 30 Jan. 1895; 11 Feb. 1895; 10 April 1895.
[4] *Minutes*, 18 Feb. 1895.
[5] *Ibid.* 1 June 1895. The Town Council's contribution was £25. The
balance of about £150 left over was retained by the Trades Council until
required for a similar purpose in the future.

narrowly-based Parochial Boards which administered poor
relief in those Scottish parishes which adopted compulsory
assessment, but by the Local Government (Scotland) Act of
1894 these Boards were replaced by Parish Councils, to be
elected on a relatively democratic franchise. At the same
time, the Aberdeen Town Council took advantage of the
Act to secure the amalgamation of the two existing parishes
in Aberdeen. This step was warmly supported by the Trades
Council, partly because it was logical, administratively
convenient, and economical to have the parish wards
identical with those used for municipal and School Board
purposes and partly because it would equalise poor-rates
between the east- and west-ends of the city and would
remove certain anomalies arising from settlement laws:
for example, 'a man might be 25 years in Aberdeen
paying rates and yet fail to get a settlement because he had
not lived in any one parish for a sufficient time. In such a
case a man when in need might have to make a claim
on a parish he had left 25 [years] before and naturally
enough that parish would likely make an endeavour to give
the applicant as little as possible.'[1]

When the first Parish Council elections were held in
Aberdeen, in 1895, the Trades Council nominated three
candidates of its own, and also recommended electors to
support three other candidates—two of whom (both members of the Trades Council) were nominees of the local
branch of the Social Democratic Federation.[2] In the programme drawn up by the Council for its candidates, the
main points were demands for the extension of outdoor relief
to the poor, that married couples be not separated on
accepting indoor relief, and that 'Parliament be asked to
extend the powers of the Parish Councils to enable them to
give relief to all poor and destitute persons and to abolish
political disqualification on the acceptance of poor relief';

---

[1] *Minutes*, 24 Oct. 1894. Before the amalgamation, the St. Nicholas municipal ward included parts of both parishes; and parish-rates were lower in
the west-end of Aberdeen than in the poorer east-end.
[2] *Ibid.* 6 Mar. 1895; *Daily Free Press*, 3 April 1895.

during the election campaign, Robertson, one of the S.D.F. candidates, claimed that all the items in this programme had first been put forward by his party.[1] In the outcome, only one of the Trades Council candidates, and neither of the S.D.F. candidates, was elected to the Parish Council. There was nothing surprising about the Trades Council's participation in these elections of 1895: by then it had become customary for it to take part in elections to all the more important governing bodies. But the next elections for the Parish Council, three years later, coincided in time with the Town Council elections, and the Trades Council was faced with the choice of either dividing its forces between the two sets of elections or of concentrating on one of them: it chose to take no part in the municipal elections but to nominate three candidates for the Parish Council. Two of these candidates were successful, as was one of the two S.D.F. candidates in that year.[2]

It is obvious enough that the recurrent unemployment of the mid-'eighties and the early 'nineties had, at the time, important effects on working-class organisations in Aberdeen. But there had been an even more important development in the intervening period, in the late 'eighties: the movement for the working day to be limited by statute to eight hours. Throughout Britain, the unemployment and increasing intensity of labour in the 'eighties was reflected in a growing demand for an eight-hour working day. At the same time, British Socialists, few in number and relatively isolated from the working-class, had to solve the problem of building up an independent political party—with its own programme—based on parliamentary action and drawing on trade unionists for support. The solution of the problem, the means of establishing a link between Socialists and the main body of trade unionists, was seen by more far-sighted Socialists in a campaign for a statutory eight-hour day. Tom

[1] Minutes, 2 Mar. 1895; Daily Free Press, 14 Mar. 1895.
[2] Minutes, 12 Oct. 1898; Daily Free Press, 2 Nov. 1898. In part, the preference of the Trades Council for the elections to the Parish Council was probably due to the fact that that public body held its meetings in the evening—the Town Council did not.

Mann led the way in a pamphlet on the subject, published in 1886; other Socialist leaders, such as Burns, Champion, and Hardie, also put the demand for an Eight Hours Bill foremost in their programmes—and in the background was Engels, working on similar lines through Eleanor Marx-Aveling. The alliance that was forged between Socialists and important sections of trade unionists was not a one-sided one: if the Socialists, to transform their small nuclei into an effective political force, needed the support of trade unionists, the latter, unless they were to gain the eight-hour day and other aims by industrial action or through one or other of the main political parties, needed a new political party with a programme similar to that advocated by the Socialists. Since neither the Conservative nor the Liberal party was willing to agree to an eight-hour day, the debate in working-class organisations turned at first on whether the reform could be achieved by industrial action or whether recourse to Parliament would be necessary; the leaders of the older and larger craft unions tended to assert their faith in the ability of their organisations to gain the eight-hour day, when circumstances were ripe, through negotiation with employers, whilst the newer unions, conscious of their comparative industrial weakness, were more inclined to support a policy of legislative enforcement of their industrial demands and, therefore, of association with Socialists. It was, for example, no accident that the Aberdeen branch of the Scottish Farm Servants' Union, consisting largely of carters, was predominantly left-wing in outlook in the early 'nineties.

In Aberdeen, as in other parts of the country at the turn of the 'eighties, there was constant debate on the question of an eight-hour day, the Trades Council being the main forum for working-class opinion. Although there was some confusion at first as to whether an eight-hour day meant a forty-hour or a forty-eight-hour week (most members of the Council considering that it meant the latter) nearly all were agreed as to the desirability of such a reform. There was very little suggestion that such a limitation of working hours would, in effect, be a disguised form of wage-increase through overtime pay: throughout, it was conceived almost entirely as a means of abolishing unemployment or at least of spreading it more evenly and lightly. Thus, A. Catto moved in the Trades Council 'that it was expedient to ask for a reduction of the working hours to Eight Hours a day', and argued that an eight-hour day 'would do much to provide employment for those at present unemployed by increasing the demand for labour';[1] the *Aberdeen Labour Elector* observed in 1893 that 'There are at this moment in Aberdeen about 1,000 men out of employment. . . . To that we have only one reply: the legislative eight-hours day. In spite of the superior wisdom of party hacks and Socialist sucklings we adhere to our remedy which is, in truth, not a palliative but a panacea';[2] and two years later the Trades Council resolved 'in view of the large and increasing number of workers continually out of employment . . . to make the shortening of the hours of labour by legal enactment the test question at next general election'.[3]

Time after time in 1888-9 the Trades Council discussed the means whereby an eight-hour day might be gained. P. Milne, a blacksmiths' delegate and a staunch individualist Liberal, was the main opponent of a statutory limitation of hours: at first, he was inclined to oppose the very idea of a reduction of working hours,[4] but he found himself isolated on that point and proceeded to outline his real objections to a statutory eight-hour day. 'In his opinion it was too small a matter to require the intervention of the State, and even though such a Bill as proposed was passed he doubted very much if it would find work for the unemployed, or relieve the distress of the people to any great extent'; and Milne concluded his argument by roundly declaring that 'the "State" had been asked to interfere too much already and he for one declined to sell his liberty for such a Mess of

[1] *Minutes*, 18 Jan. 1888. The motion was carried by sixteen votes to one.
[2] *Aberdeen Labour Elector*, 21 Jan. 1893. 'Socialist sucklings' refers to the (Marxist) Aberdeen Socialist Society which strongly advocated a statutory limitation of hours of work but regarded such a reform as one of a number of 'palliatives of existing social evils' (*The Workers' Herald*, 12 Dec. 1891).
[3] *Minutes*, 1 May 1895; 3 July 1895.   [4] *Ibid.* 23 Nov. 1887.

Pottage as an Eight Hours Bill'.[1] But Milne's oratory was unavailing; early in 1888 the Trades Council resolved 'that the Eight Hours be got by legislation', rejecting by a majority of seventeen to three an amendment 'that the Eight Hours be got by the voluntary effort of the organised trades unions throughout the Kingdom'.[2]

This resolution was not decisive, and in 1889, when it was necessary to instruct the Trades Council delegates to the Trades Union Congress, the whole question of the eight-hour day was reopened. This time 'it was unanimously agreed that such a day should be wrought',[3] but Milne again opposed a motion favouring the achieving of an eight-hour day by legislative enactment, arguing that 'those in favour of the movement sought to make the State omnipotent'. However, the motion was carried by an overwhelming majority—thirty-two to three—and the delegates to the T.U.C. were instructed accordingly on this issue;[4] moreover, 'So strong are the opinions of the Council on this question that the Delegates were instructed not to support Mr. Broadhurst as Parliamentary Secretary, owing to the views he held in regard to it'.[5] Those opinions were indeed strongly held, as was shown shortly afterwards. At the T.U.C., held in Dundee in 1889, Keir Hardie's motion in favour of a statutory eight-hour day was defeated[6]—but the Aberdeen Trades Council was more immediately concerned with the

---

[1] *Minutes*, 18 Jan. 1888. Implicit in this argument was the fear of some trade unionists that State intervention in the question of working hours (of male adults, as distinct from the hours of women and children on which legislation already existed) would establish a precedent for State intervention in other matters, e.g. wages, not necessarily to the advantage of workers.

[2] *Ibid.* 1 Feb. 1888. This was at a time when the Edinburgh Trades Council, for example, still preferred to rely on industrial pressure (W. H. Marwick, *op. cit.* p. 159).

[3] *Ibid.* 26 June 1889.　　　　　　　[4] *Ibid.* 21 Aug. 1889.

[5] *Annual Report* of Aberdeen United Trades Council for 1889 (in Aberdeen Public Library). Broadhurst, secretary of the Parliamentary Committee of the T.U.C., had opposed the miners' eight-hours Bill in Parliament.

[6] Partly because it did not meet the interests of all workers. For example, the Scottish miners, whose unions were weak, supported the proposal, whereas the strongly-organised miners of Durham and Northumberland did not— they were already working a seven-hour day.

fact that only one of its four delegates had voted against Broadhurst in a vote of confidence on the latter, the other three delegates having abstained. When the delegates returned to Aberdeen, the three who had abstained were questioned as to why they had not honoured their mandate. On the defensive, they quibbled: their specific instructions had been simply to oppose Broadhurst's re-appointment to the secretaryship of the Parliamentary Committee. The Trades Council was not satisfied with this explanation and declared in a resolution that the three delegates, in the matter of their vote on Broadhurst at the T.U.C., 'did not represent this Council'.[1] The measure of the Council's indignation may be gauged from the fact that the repudiated delegates were important figures in the Council—two of them, Livingston and Keir, were respectively president and vice-president at the time.

Amongst the trade unions in Aberdeen which can be distinguished as supporting the legal eight-hour day proposal in 1888-90 were those of the ironmoulders, shipwrights, shore labourers, seamen and firemen, stonepolishers, Scottish operative tailors, printers, and bakers—it was at the instigation of the Aberdeen branch that the Scottish Bakers' Federal Union was soon to agitate for a separate eight-hours Bill to meet its special case. The apparent completeness of the acceptance of the legal eight-hour day idea by the craftsmen of Aberdeen gives food for thought as to whether many of the national leaders of the craft-unions, so prominent in their opposition to the idea at the T.U.C., were really aware —or wished to be aware—of the views of the ordinary members of their organisations on the subject. Indeed, it seems that the only union in Aberdeen which at all strongly opposed a statutory eight-hour day was that of the Associated Carpenters, which was then—but not for long—the stronger of the two carpenters' unions in the city: for the

[1] *Minutes*, 18 Sep. 1889; 2 Oct. 1889; 16 Oct. 1889. In the whole period under consideration, there was no other instance of the Council repudiating delegates; perhaps this one sharp and salutary lesson in the elements of democracy was all that was necessary.

rest, opposition came only from a few individual Liberals, such as P. Milne[1] and W. Livingston. It may be that some other local trade union leaders still had inward misgivings in 1889,[2] but if so, such doubts were swamped in the following year. To celebrate the first May Day, the Trades Council decided to organise a march and demonstration in favour of a legal eight-hour day; it also decided, against the opposition of McHardy (of the Associated Joiners) and Milne, to invite Burns, Mann, and Tillett to speak at the demonstration.[3] As preparations were advanced, enthusiasm rose; and when Peter Milne was asked, ' "What about the blacksmiths?" he rose and said heartily, "If ye're a' to be demonstratin' in favour o' an aicht-oors day, Aw'm gaun' to demonstrate tee!" . . . Such is the power of suggestion and the attraction of the crowd.'[4] The demonstration turned out to be a great success, between 10,000 and 15,000 people being present.[5]

After this signal demonstration of the popular appeal of a legal eight-hour day, there was very little further opposition to the proposal in the Trades Council: not only were the delegates to the T.U.C. in 1890 instructed to support the proposal, but it was decided to distribute pamphlets on the subject amongst other delegates;[6] and the Trades Council programme for the municipal elections of 1890 included a claim for an eight-hour day for employees of the Town

[1] Milne was secretary of the Aberdeen branch of the Associated Blacksmiths' Society, as well as being a delegate to the Trades Council, but his views on the eight-hour day did not necessarily represent those of his brother-blacksmiths: W. Johnston, another blacksmiths' delegate, supported a legal eight-hour day.
[2] Leatham says that he and other Socialists who were members of the Trades Council 'rather rushed the old-fashioned trade unionists politically' at about this time (J. Leatham, loc. cit. vol. XXIX, no. 342, p. 17).
[3] Minutes, 19 Mar. 1890; 2 April 1890; 16 April 1890; 30 April 1890. Burns, Mann, and Tillett were unable to come to Aberdeen for the demonstration; H. H. Champion came instead.
[4] J. Leatham, loc. cit. vol. XXIX, no. 342, p. 17.
[5] Daily Free Press, 19 May 1890.
[6] Minutes, 20 Aug. 1890. It was at this T.U.C. meeting that the legal eight-hour day motion was carried, and Broadhurst resigned the secretaryship of the Parliamentary Committee.

7

Council.[1] Peter Milne, it is true, recovered from his May Day lapse and trod once more the paths of rugged individualism—in 1894 he was opposing an eight-hour day for Town Council employees because he did not wish them to be 'too much pampered' and because 'when men entered the service of the Town Council they invariably deserted their Union'![2]—but few people were inclined to take him very seriously on such matters, well-liked and respected though he was.

Some groups of workers in Aberdeen secured a shorter working week in the eighteen-nineties: for instance, sawmillers had their hours reduced from fifty-six to fifty-four; bakers gained a reduction of three hours; and quarrymen also worked a shorter week. But the eight-hour day was not achieved by most workers for very many years, and superficially the campaign for it seems to have been a failure, the demand becoming one of the hoary annuals at successive Trade Union Congresses. In reality, however, the campaign for a statutory eight-hour day—and the unemployment which largely provoked it—was of exceptional importance because of its political implications: a theme which is best considered in relation to more directly political matters. At this point, it must suffice to point out that unemployment and the legal eight-hour day campaign were inextricably connected with the upsurge and political ferment in working-class circles in Aberdeen at the turn of the 'eighties.

Some of the economic and social factors which affected trade unionism in the Great Depression have now been considered—questions of wages, technical change and intensity of labour, and unemployment—and others, such as the intangible effects of more widespread education, obviously have their importance. Yet such developments

[1] *Minutes*, 10 Oct. 1890.
[2] *Ibid.* 28 Mar. 1894. W. Diack (*op. cit.* pp. 154-5) gives an amusing illustration of Milne's pawky humour. Milne, after being pressed as to his views on Socialism once 'said something like this: "Weel weel! I've tell't ye fat I think o' yer Socialism. Maybe I'm ower auld to cheenge—but I'll just add ae ither wird: I hae fower sons an' fower dothers, an' they're a' Socialists. . . . Gin ye a' dae as weel for Socialism——." '

impinged upon the consciousness of individual men and women, upon people with well-established and traditional sets of values and ideas, and the slowness with which such ideas are usually upset or modified is notorious. The response which economic and social development did in fact evoke was in no way inevitable: such response developed within the framework of, and was partly based upon, existing ideas; and its speed of growth depended particularly upon the degree to which a sufficient number of able men, preferably working together in an organised manner, were prepared to foster it and provide leadership. To take one illustration, it has been shown that the degree of unemployment in Aberdeen was smaller than in very many other industrial centres of Britain in the mid-'eighties, yet the working-class reaction to it, as expressed in the eight-hour day campaign, was at least as marked in Aberdeen as in any other area and more so than in most. Similarly, the exceptional rapidity with which new political ideas and modes of action spread and were seized upon by ever-growing numbers of people, especially working-class people, in Aberdeen in the 'eighties and 'nineties, cannot be understood without taking full account of the remarkably capable body of men who led the trade union movement in Aberdeen. They made mistakes, and few of them left their mark on national trade union or political life; but taken together they constituted a powerful and live force in Aberdeen. Their personal ability and drive are demonstrated by the record of presidents of the Trades Council, of whom there were eight in the nineteen years between 1882 and 1900: of these eight men, two—Elphinstone and Robertson—emigrated during their terms of office; Thompson became a newsagent; Bisset and Livingston subsequently founded their own businesses and became employers; Elrick was foreman of a big granite yard; Nicol was foreman of the largest bindery in the north of Scotland; and Keir, a blind man, was a foreman basket-maker. Moreover, these men achieved their personal positions only by dint of their own ability: they were not 'bought' in any sense.

PART IV

POLITICS

CHAPTER VII

LIBERALISM IN THE 'EIGHTIES

THE years of the eighteen-eighties were marked by a profound ferment of social and political ideas and activities, affecting all classes of the community in Britain. The negative doctrine of economic individualism was challenged by more positive concepts of social organisation. On the one hand, for the first time in decades, there was serious questioning of the tenets of free trade:[1] as other countries, particularly Germany and the U.S.A., emerged as industrial rivals; as British exporters were challenged by foreigners in neutral markets (and even, in some commodities, in the British market itself); as foreign tariff-barriers and export-bounties mounted higher; so those British industrial interests which were particularly affected—such as sugar, silks, worsteds—began to promote a campaign for protection, albeit thinly disguised as 'fair trade'. The campaign was promoted in conjunction with landed interests which were concerned by the growing flood of food-imports, and, with its accompanying emphasis on empire and imperial preference, it came to be identified with the Conservative party ; attempts to enlist working-class support for 'fair trade' were failures on the whole, though occasion will arise later in this survey to refer to some inclination of workers in Aberdeen towards Conservative policy in this respect.

On the other hand, there was dissatisfaction amongst many working-class and lower middle-class people with the social effects of *laissez-faire* capitalism. To the law of the market and the social atomism of economic liberalism were now counterposed new, more humanitarian, criteria of social values, revolving around the need for more State intervention: even to those with no personal experience of

[1] Cf. B. H. Brown, *The Tariff Reform Movement in Great Britain 1881-1895* (1943).

poverty, social disturbance and investigation were bringing home the realisation that it could not be assumed that increased production would, of itself, eliminate large-scale poverty and its effects. Naturally, the centre of interest in this development of ideas was the Liberal party, the fount of economic individualism and the party traditionally supported by most workers. Both before and after the split over Irish Home Rule in the 'eighties, the Liberal party was visibly torn by conflicting stresses and pressures: conflict between its Whig and Radical sections, and the underlying conflict between the working-class and middle-class adherents of the party—the latter conflict being entangled with the former, since the Radicals included, and were mainly led by, advanced employers. To some extent, pressure from within the party by Radical workers was successfully headed off: the caucus was developed, partly as an expression of Radical opposition to Whig leadership, partly in response to the changed conditions resulting from the extension of the franchise to artisans in the towns under the Act of 1867; a number of working-men were adopted as candidates, and some were elected as Liberal M.P.s; and, in 1886, Broadhurst was brought into the Liberal administration as an Under-Secretary of State—an appointment which prompted the Aberdeen Trades Council to congratulate Broadhurst, 'he being the first bona fide working man upon [whom] such an honour has ever been conferred'.[1]

Yet the record of the Liberal administration of 1880-5 was far from satisfactory to Radicals, and disillusionment spread. With Radicalism barely represented in the Cabinet, very little social legislation was enacted, apart from a useful but limited Employers' Liability Act and an important Irish Land Act—and the latter was virtually forced upon Gladstone by the incipient revolutionary situation in Ireland. Nevertheless, if the Liberal panaceas of the 'eighties were mainly political, not social, in content, there were still

---

[1] *Minutes*, 17 Feb. 1886. The Council had previously been gratified at the appointment of W. J. Davis, of Birmingham, as a factory inspector, 'he being a Workingman' (*Minutes*, 7 Feb. 1883).

strong grounds for the attachment of workers to Liberalism and, more specifically, to Radicalism. The Radical tradition of sturdy individualism and suspicion of government and imperialism, of independence and assertion of civil liberties, of hostility to landowners, and belief in the benefits of popular education, was deep-rooted and made a strong appeal. These various strands were often entwined with one another, as in the case of Irish and Scottish Home Rule, and the strength of their appeal may be illustrated from some of the matters in which the Aberdeen Trades Council took an interest.

The crofting question was at its height in the 'eighties, and the Trades Council frequently manifested its hostility to landowners and its desire for land-law reform. For example, it refused to express support for the idea of state-directed emigration, basing its refusal partly on grounds of disapproval of the principle of state intervention and partly on the contention that 'the present condition of things is the result of bad legislation, and that it is the duty of the State to make a thorough and radical reform in our land and other laws calculated to ameliorate the condition of the people'.[1] More specifically, the Trades Council on another occasion suggested a reform of land-laws to make it compulsory upon all owners to cultivate 'all lands capable of producing food for the people', and urged the removal of all obstacles in the way of an extension of peasant-proprietorship.[2] The Council favoured the extension of Highland crofting legislation to the whole of Scotland,[3] and was indignant at severe terms of punishment meted out by courts to a number of Lewis crofters;[4] and, coming nearer home, in 1889 it went to considerable lengths in support of squatters who were protesting at the action of a number of

---

[1] *Minutes*, 21 Nov. 1883. The Council vacillated on the question of State-aided emigration, supporting the idea on 9 June 1886 and again opposing it on 31 Oct. 1888.

[2] *Ibid.* 17 June 1884. In this debate there was some expression of opinion in favour of land-nationalisation. By 1893, if not before, the Council was advocating nationalisation of the land (*Minutes*, 27 Sep. 1893).

[3] *Ibid.* 17 Mar. 1886.   [4] *Ibid.* 15 Feb. 1888.

lairds who had enclosed and apportioned amongst themselves the hill of Bennachie in Aberdeenshire—the Council ceased its activity on this issue only after being advised by the professional searcher of records engaged by it that the lairds concerned had acted within their rights from a legal point of view.[1]

Meanwhile, the Trades Council had defined its position in relation to Irish affairs, involving associated problems of land, national independence, and civil liberties. In a debate in 1881 on the Irish Land Bill, some anti-Irish feeling was expressed, several delegates contending that 'in a great measure the chief obstacles to any material or satisfactory improvement in the condition of the people of Ireland lay in certain natural defects incident to their race'. Other delegates contested this view, claiming that, in Ireland, 'the old feudal laws . . . had been the means of keeping the people in a state of ignorance and subjection, and further that a system of agency and landlord absenteeism connected with land had drained the country of that wealth which was necessary to increase its value and for the creation and development of other industries for the employment of the inhabitants'. The debate was concluded by a unanimous expression of support for the Irish Land Bill.[2]

In 1886, the Council expressed its approval of Gladstone's Irish Home Rule and Land Purchase Bills,[3] and in the following year it protested on three separate occasions at repressive measures in Ireland: for example, it condemned 'the attempted suppression of the right of public meeting and freedom of speech in Ireland, . . . and the murderous attack on defenceless people at Mitchelstown', Bisset, the president, declaring that it 'would ill become them as Trades Unionists to hesitate for a single minute in expressing sympathy with their Irish brethren in resisting the yoke of tyranny and injustice under which they laboured'.[4] The

---

[1] W. Diack, op. cit. pp. 93-6; Minutes, 11 June 1890.
[2] Ibid. 4 May 1881. There was no Irish colony in Aberdeen.
[3] Ibid. 13 May 1886.
[4] Ibid. 28 Sep. 1887. See also ibid. 27 April 1887; 7 Dec. 1887.

question of Home Rule for Ireland was seen in a very broad context: 'in view of the resolution lately passed by this Council in favour of Home Rule for Ireland and believing that on these lines lie the solution of the question of Local Government, the federation of the Colonies with Great Britain, and the Abolition of the House of Lords, we hereby declare in favour of Home Rule for Scotland. Also that it be remitted to the executive along with other associations or individuals to endeavour to establish a Branch of the Scottish Home Rule Association in Aberdeen.'[1]

As in the case of Scots crofters and Irish peasants, so in other matters concerning political liberty the Trades Council was seldom slow to register its support for extensions of democracy or its opposition to restrictions upon it. A few examples must suffice: in conjunction with the Liberal Association, the Council participated in the campaign of demonstrations and petitions in favour of extending the franchise in 1884—and in condemnation of the opposition of the House of Lords;[2] it constantly urged an extension of the hours of polling in elections;[3] requested local M.P.s to endeavour to have the law of conspiracy so amended as 'to provide against any misinterpretation [by the courts] of the Act in future';[4] and protested vigorously against the use of troops in connection with strikes of dockers at Hull and miners at Featherstone in Yorkshire.[5] Most typical, perhaps, was the attitude of the Council towards the local police force, which was critically observed to ensure that it did not exceed its duties: there was condemnation of the action of the superintendent of police in interfering with an open-air Socialist meeting held on a Sunday, and later there was sustained criticism of what was alleged to be unnecessary officiousness by the police in their treatment of arrested

---

[1] *Minutes*, 7 July 1886. This motion was carried unanimously. The Trades Council also favoured the disestablishment and disendowment of the Church of Scotland (29 June 1885).

[2] *Ibid.* 23 April 1884; 9 July 1884; 16 July 1884; 13 Aug. 1884.

[3] E.g. *Minutes*, 20 Mar. 1878; 13 Feb. 1884.

[4] *Ibid.* 4 Feb. 1891.

[5] *Ibid.* 12 April 1893; 27 Sep. 1893.

persons.[1] This culminated in an expression of the Council's opinion that 'the only permanent remedy for the dissatisfaction with the police is to put them under the control of the Local Authority'.[2]

Finally, in this survey of the appeal of the Radical tradition to the working-class in Aberdeen, it is worth glancing at the interest shown by the Trades Council in educational matters. The Scottish Education Act came into operation in 1873, but seven years later the Council was unanimously of the opinion that the educational system 'as contrasted with the system in practice previous to the Act of 1872 both as regards results and costs is much less satisfactory'.[3] Apart from its interest in School Board elections, the Council frequently considered educational matters in the 'eighties. Sometimes the questions under discussion were relatively minor ones, such as objections to 'cramming'[4] and the lack of uniformity of school text-books; more often the Council was concerned to point to the necessity of abolishing school fees or at least, as a first step, of reducing them. The advocacy of free education was expressed consistently by the Council from 1881—its delegates to the T.U.C. in 1885 were instructed to raise the question there—and a powerful ally was found in W. Hunter, Radical M.P. for North Aberdeen from 1885 to 1896: Hunter's main concern, inside and outside Parliament, was to press for free education, and it was this more than anything else that secured for him the lasting respect and support of trade unionists in Aberdeen. By the early 'nineties, the struggle for free education had been virtually won,[5] and the emphasis of the Trades Council's educational policy was placed on other desirable reforms: the

---

[1] *Minutes*, 21 Aug. 1889; 12 April 1893; 26 April 1893. See also J. Leatham, *loc. cit.* vol. XXVIII, no. 329, pp. 18-20; vol. XXVIII, no. 330, pp. 10-17.

[2] *Ibid.* 24 May 1893.   [3] *Ibid.* 13 Oct. 1880.

[4] Shanks, a cabinetmakers' delegate, contended that 'the present system of teaching was superficial and not calculated to be for the best interests of the pupils, the understanding being sacrificed in order to obtain results which were beyond the average capacity of the pupils' (*Minutes*, 1 Aug. 1883).

[5] By 1893, fees were being charged at only three elementary schools, so that all but 18 per cent. of the children in Aberdeen were receiving free education.

raising of the school-leaving age, the provision of technical and secondary education, and the supplying of free books.[1]

Needless to say, the Trades Council was by no means the only organisation pursuing a fundamentally Radical policy in Aberdeen in the 'eighties. There was, for example, a Land-law Reform Association, which was virtually a Liberal body. The Council usually co-operated with such bodies on particular issues and sometimes deferred to their leadership, as in the case of the Lewis crofters in 1888 and the franchise campaign of a few years earlier. On other occasions, particularly in the latter part of the decade, the Council was inclined to take the lead itself, prodding Liberal organisations into activity: Bisset, its president, was said to have been instrumental, in 1886, in 'causing one or more of our large associations to declare their policy both upon Home Rule for Scotland and for Ireland'.[2]

Aberdeen was noted as a Radical stronghold: it was represented in Parliament by Liberals before 1885, and from that date, when the city was divided into two constituencies, it returned two Liberal M.P.s without a break until 1918. There was naturally a Conservative party organisation in the city in the 'eighties, drawing its main strength from local landowners, estate-agents and lawyers,[3] but it was not very effective; and a Conservative Working Men's Association existed for several years but did not gain any substantial support amongst workers.[4] The Liberal party, on the other hand, enjoyed the support not only of most workers but also

---

[1] E.g. *Minutes*, 27 May 1891; 19 Aug. 1891; 25 Aug. 1897.

[2] *Daily Free Press*, 26 April 1888. The 'large associations' referred to were probably the Liberal Association and the Junior Liberal Association.

[3] '. . . even in this radical city of Aberdeen, I find that out of one hundred and six advocates, no less than seventy are Conservatives' (Aberdeen Working Men's Conservative Association, *Address by A. Forbes on Political Principles versus Practice* [pamphlet, Aberdeen Public Library]).

[4] Although the platform of the Association, at public meetings, was usually overwhelmingly weighted with local lairds, the chairman was W. Leys, who was also a blacksmiths' delegate to the Trades Council. Leys invariably found himself isolated in the Trades Council, as in 1887 when he wished to move the previous question against the motion condemning the incident at Mitchelstown: he failed to secure a seconder.

of most employers, including such influential figures as P. Esslemont, the big draper and M.P. for East Aberdeenshire, J. W. Crombie of the Grandholm woollen mill, A. H. Wilson, of Hall, Russell and Company, shipbuilders, and the Davidson and Pirie families, paper-mill owners.[1] Indeed, so strong was Liberalism in the city that for the greater part of the last two decades of the nineteenth century the Aberdeen Liberal Association could afford the luxury of not openly participating in local government elections (though there was wire-pulling behind the scenes, and no doubt the fact that a particular 'independent' candidate was known to be a Liberal was a strong recommendation), and this sometimes resulted in the anomaly of a Conservative Lord Provost presiding over a Town Council composed largely of Liberals. Even the schism in the party in 1886, over the question of Irish Home Rule, did not greatly affect the local Liberal Association: the organisation remained firmly Gladstonian and few of its leaders broke away as Liberal Unionists, though the defection of the *Daily Free Press* was a serious matter.

If Liberal organisations were so influential in Aberdeen in the 'eighties, it was partly at least due to their own activity; and the forms taken by that activity were not always to the liking of the more prominent local leaders of the party. The Aberdeen Liberal Association was formed in the spring of 1877, and was based upon the usual Birmingham model of ward committees, a very large city council consisting of representatives from the wards, and an executive committee. On the whole, the organisation seems to have been dominated by Gladstonian moderates—they could not accurately be described as either Whigs or Radicals—but there was ample room for the expression of differing viewpoints within the association: for instance, three members of the Trades Council, G. Bisset, J. C. Thompson, and J. Mackintosh, were also members of the executive committee of the Liberal Association in 1885.

[1] There were, of course, some Conservative or Liberal Unionist employers, notably the Stewart family, which owned comb-works.

Nevertheless, the radical elements were dissatisfied with the relatively slow pace set by the moderates, and several organisations sprang up alongside the Liberal Association: independent and active organisations, composed mainly of Radicals, whose chief function was to push the Liberal Association along more advanced paths without being openly hostile to it.

When Leatham wrote that 'the crusading spirit was strong in Liberalism in the 'eighties',[1] he probably had these organisations in mind, and two of them in particular are worthy of note: the Aberdeen Junior Liberal Association and the Aberdeen Radical Association. The former was established by the end of 1882, when it was agitating on the land question:[2] throughout its existence its chairman was Professor Minto, a life-long Liberal who had nevertheless strongly opposed Gladstone's policy of coercion in Ireland in 1881, and its secretary was G. Gerrie. Gerrie later wrote of the Junior Liberal Association: 'It cannot be doubted that this organisation was brought into existence for the express purpose of pulverising the local Caucus. . . . The organisation, as is well known, was for years abnormally vigorous.'[3] Vigorous and rebellious against official Liberalism the Association certainly was: one of the last public meetings it held was in the spring of 1888 when it heard Cunninghame Graham and Keir Hardie put the case for working-class politics. That meeting, according to Leatham, 'finished' the Junior Liberal Association,[4] and it became defunct: most of its leaders were advancing beyond the stage of acting as a pressure-group within Liberal party organisations.

A body with an even shorter span of life was the Aberdeen Radical Association. It was formed in 1884[5] and although

[1] J. Leatham, *loc. cit.* vol. XXVIII, no. 326, p. 12.
[2] *Daily Free Press*, 29 Dec. 1882.
[3] Obituary notice on Minto by 'Thorough' (a nom-de-plume used by Gerrie), *Aberdeen Labour Elector*, 18 Mar. 1893.
[4] J. Leatham, *loc. cit.* vol. XXVIII, no. 332, pp. 9-11, 16.
[5] There was probably an informal Radical grouping before this: a number of Radicals were apparently responsible for inviting Michael Davitt to speak in Aberdeen on Irish affairs, especially land-nationalisation, in 1882.

its president was A. Duffus, a merchant, its members and leaders were predominantly working-class—with a sprinkling of such men as W. Lindsay, who was a publisher, old Chartist, and Ruskin enthusiast. There was little difference between this association and the Junior Liberals, except that the latter attracted more middle-class professional people: the Radical Association was so obviously working-class in composition that it is not easily distinguishable from the Trades Council, with which it co-operated closely. Its greatest achievement was in successfully promoting the Radical candidature of W. Hunter for the parliamentary constituency of North Aberdeen in 1885, and within a year or two of that event the association seems to have become defunct—possibly its leaders decided that the Trades Council was a more suitable organisation for their activities. There was perhaps an echo of the organisation in 1888, when a group of men, notably Bisset, Thompson, and the Rev. Webster, organised a campaign of protest against the decision of the Town Council to offer the freedom of the city to G. J. Goschen, the Liberal Unionist Chancellor of the Exchequer;[1] but the Trades Council was probably the prime mover in this, though not officially.[2]

What was particularly significant about the Junior Liberal and the Radical Associations was their leadership, which overlapped to some extent. Prominent among the leaders of the Radical Association were G. Bisset, J. C. Thompson, A. Catto, A. T. G. Beveridge, and the Rev. A. Webster;[3] the committee of the Junior Liberal Association in 1886 included Bisset, W. C. Spence, W. L. Mackenzie, and G. Gerrie.[4] Within a few years, all these men were supporters of a policy of independent Labour representation,

---

[1] *Daily Free Press*, 15 Oct. 1888; 16 Oct. 1888; 22 Oct. 1888. The campaign, directed particularly at Goschen's support of coercion in Ireland, was successful: Goschen declined the honour because of the opposition expressed in Aberdeen (the Town Council itself had been very evenly divided on the matter).

[2] *Minutes*, 18 Oct. 1888. The Council later gave a donation to help defray the expenses of an anti-Goschen demonstration (28 Nov. 1888).

[3] *Daily Free Press*, 8 June 1885.   [4] *Ibid.* 27 Oct. 1886.

and it is apparent that these short-lived Liberal groupings of the 'eighties were, to many of their active members, half-way houses on the road away from the Liberal party. The two associations were essentially expressions of dissatisfaction with orthodox Liberalism: as yet, their members saw no obvious alternative to the Liberal party—it was, after all, the traditional home of good causes—but they were groping their way towards such an alternative. With their frequent public meetings and active propaganda, these dissident Liberals contributed largely to the marked increase in political interest and activity in the 'eighties:[1] more than that, their associations provided a forum for debate, in which new ideas could be discussed and vague dissatisfaction with Liberalism crystallised into something more positive. Thus, James Leatham expounded Socialism at a series of meetings of the Junior Liberal Association in 1886-7: his views met with much opposition but, according to his own account, he succeeded in winning a considerable measure of agreement from many of the Junior Liberals.[2] Socialism was one alternative to Liberalism, though it was not in fact the alternative chosen by most discontented Liberals.

[1] Other organisations also contributed. There was, for example, the Aberdeen Parliamentary Debating Society, established in 1881. As its name implies, it was modelled on Parliament and was not a party organisation, but it played a part in the formation of public opinion—as when it decided, by a vote of forty to nineteen, 'That private ownership of land is a usurpation of the common property of mankind' (*Daily Free Press*, 2 Mar. 1882). W. S. Rennie, a member of this society, became an ardent Socialist in the late 'eighties.

[2] J. Leatham, *loc. cit.* vol. XXVIII, no. 329, pp. 16-17.

CHAPTER VIII

SOCIALISM IN THE 'EIGHTIES

THE premier British Socialist organisation in the 'eighties was the Social Democratic Federation, of which the Scottish Land and Labour League constituted itself a Scottish section. At the end of 1884, William Morris and most of the members of the executive committee of the S.D.F. broke away, partly in opposition to H. M. Hyndman's dictatorial tendencies and partly because they did not favour electoral activity, and formed the Socialist League: the Scottish Land and Labour League also seceded from the S.D.F. to affiliate itself to the Socialist League.[1] A further development took place in 1888, when the Scottish Labour party was formed following Keir Hardie's unsuccessful candidature in the mid-Lanark constituency. The party was not specifically Socialist: its programme consisted of Radical political items and demands for labour legislation of an advanced character, including the eight-hour day. It was far from being a homogeneous body, since it embraced a curious mixture of elements—Radicals, Socialists, Irish Nationalists, Ruskinites, land reformers—and its form of organisation provided not only for subordinate branches but also for the affiliation of independent bodies. The Scottish Land and Labour League,[2] then the principal Socialist organisation in Scotland—it had half a dozen branches—joined the new party.

Political and personal differences hindered the Scottish Labour party from making much real progress in the following years and it dissolved itself into the Independent Labour

[1] Cf. H. W. Lee and E. Archbold, *Social Democracy in Britain* (1936), *passim*. Branches of the S.D.F. continued in existence after 1884 in Glasgow and Edinburgh; in the latter city a Scottish Socialist Federation was established in 1885 to co-ordinate the activities of members of the S.D.F. and the Socialist League.

[2] J. L. Mahon, its organiser, had been among those who had assisted Hardie in his mid-Lanark campaign.

party in 1894. Its strength had lain almost entirely in the west of Scotland, and no branch was established in Aberdeen: Keir Hardie, as secretary, offered to send a deputation to explain the objects of the Scottish Labour party to the Aberdeen Trades Council, and the offer was accepted,[1] but no such deputation ever came to Aberdeen. Nevertheless, there was already a Socialist organisation in Aberdeen. In the autumn of 1887, J. L. Mahon, organiser of the Scottish Land and Labour League, visited the city and addressed several meetings arranged for him by J. Leatham, who was already a Socialist, and as a consequence, an Aberdeen branch of the League was established.[2] Little is known of this branch in its early years, other than that it engaged in ceaseless propaganda and that another 'strong branch' was said to have been formed in the outlying village of Peter-culter—largely inhabited by paper-workers—in 1888.[3] By 1891, the organisation in Aberdeen had transformed itself into the Aberdeen Socialist Society, a change of nomen-clature which must have seemed necessary either when the Scottish Land and Labour League dissolved itself into the Scottish Labour party, or when the Socialist League itself, falling under the control of Anarchists, disintegrated in 1890. In its turn, the Aberdeen Socialist Society decided to become a branch of the S.D.F. in 1893.[4]

Rather more is known about the Aberdeen Socialist Society than about its predecessor. The Society agitated and demonstrated in favour of land-nationalisation,[5] and was violently republican in sentiment. Incidentally, one may note in this connection a striking survival of the Chartist tradition. Robert Lowery, Chartist parliamentary candidate

---

[1] *Minutes*, 15 May 1889.

[2] J. Leatham, *loc. cit.* vol. XXVIII, no. 329, pp. 17-19.

[3] *Daily Free Press*, 16 Feb. 1888.

[4] *Aberdeen Labour Elector*, 17 Aug. 1893. A group of Anarchists broke away from the Socialist Society in 1891 to form the Aberdeen Revolutionary Socialist Federation, which did not last long. This split may well have helped the Socialist Society, which claimed a year later that it was twice as strong in numbers as it had been before the exodus of the Anarchists (*The Workers' Herald*, 19 Dec. 1891).

[5] *Minutes*, 11 Aug. 1891; 19 Aug. 1891.

for Aberdeen in 1841, said at the hustings: 'And what could they think of a Government who withheld the franchise on account of the ignorance of the people, voting, as they did, £30,000 for their education, and £75,000 for the stables of Victoria's horses?'[1] Fifty years later, at a meeting of the Aberdeen Socialist Society, 'Gallacher fired off with a stinging attack upon the Royal Family. He showed by facts and figures that the horses and dogs in the Royal stables and kennels were much better housed, and generally much better cared for, than the average working man.'[2] Lowery's speech was not printed in pamphlet form, and it is not likely that Gallacher had read the newspapers of fifty years before: in all probability, this effective piece of propaganda had been handed down by word of mouth from one generation to another.

By the winter of 1891-2, when the Socialist Society was organising constant demonstrations by the unemployed, it felt strong enough to issue a weekly newspaper, *The Workers' Herald*. The first number appeared on 12 December 1891— the same day as the first issue of Blatchford's *The Clarion*— and five more numbers of what was probably the first Socialist weekly paper in Scotland[3] were published. At that point, when sales and advertisements were falling off as a result of boycott and the fact that the paper was too advanced in its political make-up for most people, Leatham, its very competent editor, fell ill, and *The Workers' Herald* came to an abrupt end.[4] For the next two or three years, the Socialist Society was overshadowed by the newly-formed I.L.P.

It would be easy to dismiss as unimportant the Aberdeen branch of the Scottish Land and Labour League and the Aberdeen Socialist Society, and this is the more charitable explanation of the blanket of silence cast by the local press

---

[1] *Aberdeen Journal*, 7 July 1841.

[2] *The Workers' Herald*, 16 Jan. 1892. The Trades Council was also inclined towards republicanism, e.g. it condemned the action of the Town Council in giving £100 as a marriage present to the Duke of York (*Minutes*, 7 June 1893).

[3] Keir Hardie's contemporary paper, *The Miner*, was run on trade union lines.

[4] J. Leatham, *loc. cit.* vol. XXIX, no. 342, pp. 12-14.

over their activities. Their membership was very small: in 1893 the Socialist Society had thirty subscribing members.[1] Indeed, there were probably not more than about 2,000 members of Socialist organisations in the whole of Britain in the 'eighties, of whom about 1,000 were members of the S.D.F. and about 500 members of the Socialist League.[2] Yet the influence of these organisations cannot be reckoned simply in terms of their membership: what they lacked in numbers they made up for in enthusiasm and hard work. In Aberdeen, their influence is to be reckoned in terms of the part played by individual Socialists in their trade unions and in the Trades Council, for instance in support of a statutory limitation of working hours and in urging skilled workers to make common cause with unskilled: it was W. Cooper, a Socialist, who moved the Trades Council resolution of May 1890, instructing delegates from skilled trades to use their influence to persuade labourers to become trade unionists. Their influence is to be reckoned also in terms of the incalculable effects of constant propaganda.

Between 1888 and 1893 frequent visits were paid to Aberdeen by Socialist lecturers of national repute: such people as William Morris, H. M. Hyndman, Eleanor Marx-Aveling, J. Bruce Glasier, Cunninghame Graham, H. H. Champion, and H. Burrows—and others of the calibre of Kropotkin. The occasion of Morris' visit in March 1888 provided an interesting commentary on one possible effect of the strength of Radicalism in the city. Morris lectured to a small meeting of about 200 people, and later wrote in *The Commonweal* that he had found his audience 'heavy to lift', and suggested that they were 'held down by the local Radicalism'.[3] Morris may have been right; it is conceivable that the very strength of Radicalism hindered the development of Socialism in Aberdeen. On the other hand, that same strength probably had more important effects in another direction: it meant that the feasibility of

[1] *Aberdeen Labour Elector*, 17 Aug. 1893.
[2] H. M. Pelling, *op. cit.* p. 12.
[3] J. Leatham, *loc. cit.* vol. XXVIII, no. 333, pp. 11-13, 19.

8*

a third party could be considered without being bedevilled by fear on the part of Radicals of letting Conservatives slip through on a split vote in elections.

But more important than the occasional appearances of well-known lecturers was the everyday work of the local Socialists. Among these, the guiding spirit was James Leatham. Born in 1865, Leatham was apprenticed as a compositor, and at the age of sixteen he was associated with a group of Radicals who invited Michael Davitt to Aberdeen to speak on the subject of land-nationalisation. At about the same time Leatham, like many others,[1] was influenced by reading and discussing George's *Progress and Poverty*, and, a few years later, L. Grönlund's *The Co-operative Commonwealth* and E. Bellamy's *Looking Backward*. When the Aberdeen branch of the Scottish Land and Labour League was formed, Leatham threw himself into its work; by that time he had become a foreman printer, and in 1889 he took over a small printing works on his own account, giving up his seat on the Trades Council. The failure of *The Workers' Herald*, edited and printed by Leatham, virtually ruined him; he was forced to sell his business and become a journeyman printer again. As such, he soon became secretary of the Aberdeen branch of the Scottish Typographical Association and again returned to the Trades Council as a delegate. Shortly after, however, in 1893, he left Aberdeen for Manchester.[2]

In his autobiography, Leatham has given a vivid picture of the activities of the Socialist organisation in Aberdeen at

---

[1] Cf. 'If we had to assign to any one event the starting of the new current of thought, we should name the wide circulation in Great Britain of Henry George's *Progress and Poverty* during the years 1880-1882' (S. and B. Webb, *op. cit.* p. 375). George's vigorous attack was upon land revenues only, but many of his readers saw no reason for not regarding other forms of capital in a similar way. George himself addressed meetings in Aberdeen in 1884 and 1893.

[2] Cf. J. Leatham, *loc. cit. passim*. Leatham richly deserves a biographer—his autobiography was unfinished. A great admirer of William Morris, his interests were catholic, as his writings and lectures on Shakespeare's plays testify. He later returned to north-east Scotland, and was Provost of Turriff in the nineteen-thirties.

the turn of the 'eighties. 'Leatham's Lambs', as they were sometimes ironically called, usually held meetings five times a week: each Monday evening there was a members' meeting, at which business was transacted and an article or chapter of a book—such as Grönlund's *The Co-operative Commonwealth*—read and discussed; and on Saturday evenings and Sunday afternoons and evenings there were public meetings, usually held in the open, in the east-end of Aberdeen, though sometimes they were held cheekily in the ultra-respectable area of Queen's Cross. In summer, these propaganda meetings in the city were interspersed with picnic outings to surrounding villages, where meetings were held; even on these train journeys and on the station platforms the 'lambs' continued their work by singing Socialist songs. Indeed, Wednesday evenings were devoted to choir practice, and there was about these proceedings a touch of the colour, gaiety, and cultivation of the spirit of comradeship by which the *Clarion* groups were later to be distinguished. Socialist literature was on sale at meetings, and both Leatham and Diack themselves wrote pamphlets for local distribution; one of these, Leatham's *An Eight Hours Day with Ten Hours Pay, How to Get it and How to Keep it* (Aberdeen, 1890), had a sale of ten thousand copies.[1]

These activities certainly did not produce the desired effect of a large membership for the Socialist Society, although the Aberdeen branch of the S.D.F. scored some successes in local elections in the latter part of the 'nineties. Yet constant propaganda of this character must have made an appreciable, if unmeasured, contribution to the development of ideas in the late 'eighties and early 'nineties, particularly amongst working-class people: with its accent on class struggle, it was pervasive propaganda, part, or even all, of which could be accepted by those to whom it was directed without their necessarily becoming members of the

---

[1] Other local pamphlets, published in Aberdeen in the early 'nineties, were: J. Leatham, *The Only Thing That Will Do*; J. Leatham, *Was Jesus Christ a Socialist?*; W. Diack, *The Moral Effects of Socialism* (1893); W. Diack, *The Good Time Coming*.

Socialist Society. It was probably no mere coincidence that
the Trades Council showed signs of a developing class-
consciousness in the 'eighties.

The number of members of the Trades Council who
were also members of the Socialist Society or S.D.F. in the
'nineties was never large, but their influence in debate and
in organising activities was disproportionately great. They
were respected by other members of the Council as active
and able trade unionists who did their share of the work,
and if they sometimes repelled by the seriousness with which
they took their politics, that was counterbalanced by instances
of dry humour: there were few trade unionists who could
resist the appeal of a resolution formulated in such terms as
was one put forward at the Trades Council by W. G. Smith,
secretary of the bakers' union branch:

'That having regard for the urgent necessity that exists
for a scheme of adequate Old Age Pensions being instituted
in this country and taking into account the utter incapability
of those members of the governing class who profess to be
specially interested in the matter who have sat and considered the question to devise anything other than a scheme
of old age insults this Council resolve to appoint a select
committee to consider the question in all its ramifications
with the view of formulating a practicable and wholly
adequate scheme of Old Age Pensions and thereby assist
the legislators to surmount difficulties which up to the
present time have to them been insuperable.'[1]

Relations between the Trades Council and the Socialist
Society or S.D.F. were not always smooth: there was
occasional friction, as when Leatham once blundered
inexcusably by asking, in the name of both bodies, for the
use of the grounds of Gordon's College for a demonstration
in support of land-nationalisation, although the Council had
not yet decided whether to participate in such a demonstration. Rightly incensed, the Trades Council then decided
that 'while expressing sympathy with the question of land
nationalisation' it would have nothing to do with this

[1] *Minutes*, 9 Aug. 1899.

particular demonstration.[1] Usually, however, the Council was inclined to be tolerant of its rather awkward partner and the two bodies frequently co-operated, together with the Aberdeen Independent Labour Party, in election campaigns and in such matters as the establishment of a Free Book League.

In this chapter, Socialism in Aberdeen has been discussed in terms of organisations which were basically Marxist in their outlook. No doubt there were many other non-Marxist Socialists in Aberdeen in the 'nineties, but it is not easy to distinguish them clearly. One individual who did stand out as a Socialist was the Rev. Alexander Webster, Unitarian minister, chairman of the Aberdeen School Board for some years, and founder of the Aberdeen Fresh-Air Fortnight scheme for ailing children. Webster was an uncompromising independent Socialist, always ready to speak on any platform—S.D.F., I.L.P., or Trades Council—on any subject which engaged his interest, be it the Socialism of Christ or opposition to the Boer War.

The Aberdeen I.L.P. of the early 'nineties will be discussed separately, but it may be noted here that it is extremely difficult to decide the extent to which it or its members were Socialist in the accepted sense of having as their object the public ownership of the means of production, distribution, and exchange. The party's attention was concentrated almost entirely upon immediate reforms and it very rarely considered more far-reaching questions of social organisation. In the sphere of public ownership, the main concern of Dr. Beveridge, chairman of the party, was to secure the municipal ownership of public-houses and thereby control of traffic in alcoholic liquor; and J. I. Mundie, soon to be joint-secretary of the Aberdeen I.L.P., contributed a letter to *The Workers' Herald* in 1891, in which he conceded the attractiveness of Socialist promises but argued against that further development of State activity, including State regulation of industry, predicated by Socialists.[2] Other

[1] *Minutes*, 19 Aug. 1891.
[2] 'We have had enough of restrictive legislation. . . . It is not more

leading members of the party do not seem to have defined their position at all clearly on the question of public ownership.

There was often a difference of emphasis in the respective policies of the I.L.P. and S.D.F. organisations in Aberdeen on particular matters, and some of these differences, as revealed in debates in the Trades Council (where the independent Labour attitude was much stronger than the Socialist), are interesting. One such difference concerned the question of unemployment. Both parties were united in advocating a legal eight-hour day—the I.L.P. looking on this as a solution, the S.D.F. as a useful contribution to a solution—but on the question of immediate relief for the unemployed there was a divergence of views: the S.D.F. was inclined to emphasise the organising of demonstrations of the unemployed and to demand that the Town Council provide relief work such as the construction of artisans' dwellings or road improvements, whereas the inclination of independent Labour supporters was rather to get on with the more obvious task of collecting food, clothing, and money for the unemployed.[1] It was, however, a difference of emphasis only: neither view excluded the other. Again, there was some difference of opinion on the land question. In 1893, W. Proctor, who was chairman of the farm servants' union and an independent Labour supporter—though he may still have had some connection with the Liberal party —proposed that the Trades Council should urge the government to 'appoint a commission to examine the title deeds of the landholders of this country and report as to the validity of the said title deeds, as it is a notorious fact that large tracts of land have been enclosed within recent years'. But W. Cooper, a joiner and a Socialist, successfully carried an amendment: 'That no solution of the land question will ever prove satisfactory that does not entirely abolish landlordism

restriction that is wanted, but less; not less liberty, but more' (Letter from J. I. Mundie, *The Workers' Herald*, 12 Dec. 1891). Nevertheless, Mundie supported the demand for a statutory limitation of working hours.

[1] *Minutes*, 23 Jan. 1895; 30 Jan. 1895.

by putting the control of the agricultural industry in the hands of County or Parish Councils.'[1]

In a more general sense, the Aberdeen I.L.P. was less able than the S.D.F. to achieve a proper balance between social and political policy. In their revulsion against Liberal concentration on political reforms, many independent Labour men in the city were inclined to deride political reforms which had little social content in them. This attitude, though not by any means common to all members of the I.L.P., was made sharply apparent in the Trades Council when A. Catto, himself a leading advocate of independent Labour, proposed that the government be petitioned in support of the proposal of Dr. Hunter, Radical M.P., that after their first reading all Scottish Bills should be remitted for consideration by Scottish M.P.s: in effect, Hunter was suggesting a concession to the sentiment in favour of Home Rule in Scotland. Catto then accepted a suggestion from Leatham[2] that the words 'While believing that only a Parliament sitting in Edinburgh can effectively deal with Scotch business' be added to his motion, but W. Clark Mitchell, who was a joint-secretary of the Aberdeen I.L.P., opposed the motion and put an amendment: 'That this Council believing that social legislation is of more importance than mere political changes respectfully declines to petition.' In the division which followed, Catto's motion was carried, receiving forty votes against fifteen for Mitchell's amendment.[3] Many independent Labour men must have voted with Catto and the Socialists, but the *Aberdeen Labour Elector* was forthright in declaring of Catto's motion: 'In our opinion it should never have been brought before the Council by an Independent Labour man, and certainly it should not have been carried. We are informed that the Socialist contingent voted for it. That is just what we should have expected. . . .'[4]

---

[1] *Minutes*, 7 June 1893; 21 June 1893. The amendment secured twenty-one votes, against eight for Proctor's motion.

[2] The Aberdeen Socialist Society advocated 'Home Rule to all sections of the Empire'.

[3] *Minutes*, 28 Jan. 1893.

[4] *Aberdeen Labour Elector*, 28 Jan. 1893.

But if the I.L.P. showed itself dogmatic and narrow in this respect, the S.D.F. could be equally dogmatic and sectarian in other directions. This was particularly so where trade unionism was concerned. In their eagerness to demonstrate that trade unionism alone was not enough and that it must be supplemented by political activity leading to a transformation of society, Socialists used arguments and phrases which to many trade unionists implied a distrust of trade unionism and its methods, together with a failure to appreciate the views and needs of the ordinary working-man. Many people who read an article on Lord Aberdeen in *The Workers' Herald* must have wondered what the Socialists were after. The article was entitled 'He Spends their Money for Them', and accused Lord Aberdeen of hypocrisy in giving a subscription of £100 towards the cost of erecting a Salvation Army building in Aberdeen. 'Now we don't mind Lord Aberdeen taking as much out of the farmers and labourers on his estate as he can squeeze. In fact, we should prefer that he and all other landlords gave the screw another turn or two and made economic slavery perfectly intolerable. What we object to is the thrice-damnable hypocrisy and rapacity which lead men to grind the faces of that section of the poor with whom they come immediately in contact while giving donations to be expended on the poor manufactured by other thieves.'[1] No doubt the virile language of this article would commend it to some readers: other readers must have thoughtfully asked themselves whether they really wanted their own 'economic slavery' made perfectly intolerable by another turn or two of the screw.

Socialist comment on trade unionism was equally open to dual interpretation. W. S. Rennie 'spoke of the failure of strikes—of the great railway strike with which the year 1891 commenced, of the London Carpenters' and Joiners' with which it closed—and pointed to the futility of such a method of warfare';[2] but there were many trade unionists who would not have appreciated the 'futility' of their weapon of last resort. *The Comet*, organ of the Aberdeen S.D.F. in 1898,

[1] *The Workers' Herald*, 9 Jan. 1892.   [2] *Ibid.*

considered the possibility of trades federation, a project
which was then—following the failure of the big engineers'
strike—being discussed by trade unionists up and down the
country. '. . . Trades federation then is not worth the time
and trouble that is entailed in its organisation. All that it can
achieve is a slight improvement in the conditions of slavery;
it cannot make men free. . . . Let us then throw aside all
fooling with schemes of federation and voluntaryism of all
kinds. Let us use the political machinery at our disposal to
abolish masterdom and slavedom.'[1] In contrast to the
attitude typified by such pronouncements, the *Aberdeen
Labour Elector* could declare: 'We are of course ardent Trade
Unionists, but we do object to the carrying of politics into
Trade Unionism. This is fatal. Carry your Trade Unionism
into politics and we agree. This is salvation itself'[2]—a
declaration the precise meaning of which was not clear, but
which doubtless met with the approval of most trade
unionists.

Nevertheless, most Socialists in Aberdeen were active
trade unionists, and in practice they were less distrustful of
trade unionism and more concerned to strengthen it than
some of their statements might lead one to suppose. W.
Cooper, for example, a joiner who knew from experience
the difficulties arising from the existence of two separate
joiners' unions in Aberdeen,[3] asserted that 'still there is great
need for improvement in the matter of unity among the
joiners. The fact is, there are too many unions; and a kind
of competition goes on amongst them, not as to which of
them shall be the first to organise their own labour, and thus
get rid of the "boss" altogether, but as to which of them shall
be able to offer the biggest inducements in form of sick or
buried benefits.'[4]

On the whole, it seems that the Aberdeen Socialists were
less doctrinaire than their national leaders and this was

[1] *The Comet*, 25 June 1898.
[2] *Aberdeen Labour Elector*, 28 Jan. 1893.
[3] Though there was a joint committee to co-ordinate, in trade disputes,
the activities of the local branches of the two unions.
[4] *The Workers' Herald*, 19 Dec. 1891.

perhaps due to differences of social background and experience. The Socialist organisations of the 'eighties and 'nineties, excepting the I.L.P., were led, at a national level, largely by middle-class intellectuals who had little real contact with the working-men whose support they sought. In Aberdeen, on the other hand, the Socialists were themselves working-men and trade unionists almost to a man, the great majority of them being skilled workers. Information is available concerning the social status and occupation of nearly all the local Socialists who were to any degree prominent, and only three could be considered middle-class: W. N. Cameron, who was editor of the local weekly illustrated paper, *Bon-Accord*, in 1892; and two brothers, George and William Cooper,[1] who both had small businesses as jobbing joiners. All the others were working-class: J. Leatham and P. Barron were compositors; W. S. Rennie, W. Diack, J. H. Elrick, A. Robertson, and Mowat were stonemasons; A. Gray, H. Duncan, J. W. McLean, J. Green, and Barclay were shoemakers; W. G. Smith and Shepherd were bakers; A. Ritchie, a tailor; D. Palmer, a plumber; J. Hardie, an iron-driller in a shipyard; and T. Kennedy, a railway clerk.[2] Of these eighteen working-men, all but five were delegates from their unions to the Aberdeen Trades Council at one time or another in the 'nineties.

[1] William Cooper was a member of the Society of Friends. He and his brother were probably self-employed, not employers.

[2] Kennedy stood as S.D.F. candidate for North Aberdeen in the general elections of 1906 and 1910; later, he was Labour M.P. for Kirkcaldy Burghs.

CHAPTER IX

TRADES COUNCIL AND LABOUR REPRESENTATION

It would be relatively easy to trace, in the growth of such parties as the S.D.F. and the I.L.P., the development of a political concept such as that of independent Labour representation. It is less easy to study such development in trade unions, yet such a task is perhaps more rewarding, since trade unions were large organisations representative of ordinary working-men—many more of them than the S.D.F. or I.L.P. were ever to have as members—and they were not primarily concerned with politics: changes in their political attitudes, if slower in appearance than in more directly political bodies, yet reflected more accurately what ordinary working-men were thinking.

The Aberdeen Trades Council's main function was to co-ordinate the efforts of constituent trade unions to maintain and improve the conditions of their members and naturally that function was mainly exercised in industry, in direct relations between workers and employers. Nevertheless, economic considerations could not be divorced from political, and more and more the Council felt impelled to declare its attitude upon, and to participate in, political matters. To cite only the more important considerations: in national politics there was the question of legislation for an eight-hour working day; in local government there was the fact that the Town Council was itself a considerable employer of labour, both directly and indirectly, and therefore the principal target of the demand that the standard trade union rate of wages be paid; and the interest of trade unionists in education, and therefore in the activities of the School Board, has already been indicated. Moreover, individual members of the Aberdeen Trades Council often had very definite political viewpoints of their own. True, the Trades Council was

composed solely of delegates from local trade unions or trade
union branches, and in the election of such delegates
political considerations clearly played very little part:
delegates were elected not because of their politics, but
because of their trade union work. Thus, the blacksmiths'
four delegates in 1884 were ill-assorted from a political point
of view: there was W. Leys, a prominent Conservative; P.
Milne, a well-known Liberal; W. Johnston, soon to be an
independent Labour leader; and J. Smith, who had no
pronounced political views. Similarly, the printers' delegates
for several years included both J. Leatham, a Socialist, and
W. Livingston, the most prominent of all Liberal trade
unionists in the city.

But although political considerations played little part
in their election, those members of the Trades Council who
were also members of political parties naturally viewed
particular matters with a certain social and political bias, of
which they may or may not have been conscious at the time:
almost inevitably, their attitude to some questions—not only
the more obviously political questions—was coloured by
their outside associations and affiliations. This was the more
apparent since trade unionists seem to have given their
delegates a fairly free hand, except in very important
matters. Consequently, although the Trades Council was
never subservient to any political party—indeed, it jealously
guarded its independence—it is usually possible to determine,
at any particular date, what party or social philosophy most
members of the Council supported.

In the eighteen-seventies, and for most of the 'eighties,
that party was the Liberal; even in the 'eighties and 'nineties, there were never more than two or three avowed
Conservatives amongst the delegates. What is almost the
first extant minute of a Trades Council meeting records the
reading and consideration of the constitution of the newly-
formed Aberdeen Liberal Association;[1] as the latter 'wished
as many of the artisan or operative class in their ranks as
possible', a joint meeting was held which made arrangements

[1] *Minutes*, 7 Feb. 1877.

for working-class representation on the general council of the Liberal Association.[1] The close relations between the two bodies were further demonstrated two or three years later, when the Trades Council sent three representatives, in an official capacity, to attend a Liberal demonstration in Edinburgh in honour of Gladstone. The expenses of this trip were paid by Liberals outside the Trades Council, and the latter body knew of the arrangement beforehand, but no delegate objected.[2] And in the General Election of 1880, the Council unanimously declared its support for Webster, the Liberal candidate for Aberdeen.[3]

Some instances of the Radical outlook of the Trades Council in the 'eighties have been given in an earlier chapter; in a more general sense, in the early part of the decade debates in the Council were shot through and through with Liberal philosophy. Thus, 'It was also contended that legislation as far as possible should be general in its application and not in the interests of a particular class, so that it might not be said, there is one law for the rich and another for the poor'.[4] Again, when the Council considered the uncertain progress of a strike of bakers, one delegate declared that 'If the law of supply and demand was against them, they must give in, as they could not think to overcome that'; this did not pass unchallenged, however, as another delegate 'repudiated the idea of workmen recognising the law of supply and demand. No progress would ever have been made if they had waited for the operation of that law.'[5]

There was, indeed, a latent tension in the relations between the Trades Council and the local Liberal caucus, and this was brought sharply into the open in 1879. For several years the Council had taken an interest in municipal elections; it considered the list of candidates and recommended working-men to vote for certain names, usually those of Liberals. Following this course in 1879, the Council

---

[1] *Minutes*, 2 Mar. 1877. See also *Daily Free Press*, 3 Mar. 1877.
[2] *Minutes*, 5 Nov. 1879; 3 Dec. 1879.   [3] *Ibid.* 17 Mar. 1880.
[4] Discussion on whether the provisions of the law of bankruptcy should be extended to workmen. *Minutes*, 25 May 1881.
[5] *Minutes*, 23 April 1884.

9

decided to support two specified candidates in one particular ward, 'in preference to Mr. Hunter on the grounds that although he was invariably found on the Liberal side of the [Town] Council, he had proved himself on several occasions as an enemy of the working class'.[1] At the last moment, however, Hunter's opponents withdrew from the contest, and he was elected without opposition; and it was alleged that this had been arranged by some of the leading members of the Liberal Association. The Trades Council strongly objected to this alleged intrigue: 'It was pointed out that the Council had always striven in matters of this kind to act in harmony with the Liberal Association but that conduct of this kind by some of its most prominent members would be a lesson in future.'[2] It may be that this incident had some connection with the payment of expenses for Trades Council representatives attending the Gladstone demonstration two or three weeks later: 'oiling the works' is not an uncommon political operation.

Associated with friction of this kind, though more important than it, was the desire of members of the Council to see men of their own class on public bodies. This growth of class-consciousness in the 'eighties, taken in conjunction with the expansion of trade unionism, was an extremely important development. At first, it was not directly connected with differences of policy; it was rather an instinctive movement, motivated by a feeling that it was time that working-men had a share in the work of government, and that workers could be represented best by men they could trust, by men of their own class who knew their way of life and their needs. The movement was not directed specifically against the Liberal party—after all, there were a few Liberal M.P.s who were working-class—and Liberal trade unionists could, and did, participate in it, indeed lead it, without strain on their loyalty to party: it was only later, at the turn of the 'eighties, that the real implications became apparent in the form of a feeling that working-class

[1] *Minutes*, 25 Oct. 1879.
[2] *Ibid.* 5 Nov. 1879; *Daily Free Press*, 7 Nov. 1879.

representatives should be independent of both the main political parties.

Step by step, sometimes falteringly, with the growth in importance of the Trades Council went the evolution of class-feeling. One way in which it found expression was in the struggle to secure recognition of the Council by public bodies: essentially an assertion of the dignity of the Council and of the place which its members felt that they held in the community. Until the position of the Council was assured, delegates were inclined to be touchy on this question: one of them, for example, asked the chairman if he had received an invitation to a cake and wine banquet arranged by the Town Council in connection with a royal marriage, and when the chairman replied that he had been invited, the questioner 'said that was all he wanted to know, he thought they were being ignored'.[1] There were some grounds for this touchiness, however. The Trades Council played a leading part in the decision, in 1884, to establish a free public library in Aberdeen,[2] but was very dissatisfied with the composition of the library management committee appointed by the Town Council: there was only one working-man on the committee, and although he was secretary of the Trades Council he had been appointed without notification to, or consultation with, that body. The Council therefore sent a deputation to the Lord Provost to ask for increased working-class representation on the management committee of the library. 'The Provost however questioned the right of the Trades Council to represent the working-classes, and on

---

[1] *Minutes*, 22 July 1885. On the other hand, other delegates were more concerned with the question of whether the Trades Council should countenance such municipal banquets, invitation or no invitation: most of them were opposed on principle, considering them unnecessary extravagances (*Minutes*, 5 Aug. 1885; 27 Aug. 1884).

[2] Cf. W. Diack, *op. cit.* pp. 81-2; *Minutes*, 24 May 1882; 24 Oct. 1883; 5 Dec. 1883. A majority decision at a public meeting of ratepayers was necessary to compel the Town Council to adopt the free public library Acts. One such meeting in 1882 returned a negative vote, and a campaign was necessary to procure an affirmative vote at a further meeting in 1884. The Trades Council cherished this achievement: on 20 February 1889, it contributed £25 towards the cost of a new building for the library.

being asked to name some other institution who did, referred to the working-men's conservative association, and Good Templar Lodges. In reply to that the deputation stated that the bodies named had no standing on a question of this kind, and that on any question the Town Council were promoting in which they required the assistance of the working-classes, it was to the Trades Council they looked for that assistance. Ultimately, the Provost stated that in the meantime he could do nothing. . . .'[1] Gratuitous insults of this kind only made the Trades Council more self-assertive.

The most obvious expression of class-consciousness was in connection with elections to public bodies. Already, in 1878, the Trades Council's delegate to the T.U.C. was being instructed to 'give special support to the question of increased representation of labour in Parliament',[2] but naturally the movement to implement the policy of working-class representation developed first on a local scale, in relation to such bodies as the Town Council and the School Board. A preliminary step forward was taken in 1882, when the Aberdeen School Board was due for re-election. Hitherto, the School Board had virtually been appointed by private arrangement between a Church of Scotland group and dissenting church groups; in the absence of other candidates, a poll was avoided. But the Trades Council disliked this clerical dominance and had views of its own on education, and it therefore convened a meeting, to which unaffiliated trade unions were invited, to consider the forthcoming elections. Several speakers at this meeting expressed a desire for working-class candidates, but to this there were two big stumbling-blocks: one was the difficulty of finding such candidates, since the School Board held its meetings during the day, not in the evening. The other difficulty, more important at the time, was emphasised by J. C. Thompson:

---

[1] *Minutes*, 5 June 1884. The Lord Provost also bracketed the Incorporated Trades, a masters' organisation, along with the Conservative Working Men's Association and the temperance bodies as being more representative of the working-classes than the Trades Council (*Daily Free Press*, 5 June 1884).

[2] *Minutes*, 4 Sep. 1878.

'He thought it would be unwise to press purely working-men candidates. If they could get a few popular men like Mr. Macdonald, they would get in the thin end of the wedge, and carry their point much better. They could not count upon the working men to back the candidates put forward by that meeting or by the Trades Council.'[1] This sober assessment of the state of working-class opinion was accepted: no working-men were proposed as candidates, but the Trades Council itself nominated two middle-class men, Macdonald and Brebner. To avoid a poll, the church parties then withdrew two of their candidates, and Macdonald and Brebner were consequently elected to the School Board without opposition.[2]

Two years later, the feeling that working-class opinion in Aberdeen was not yet ripe, at any rate for a working-man parliamentary candidate, was still widespread. Webster, the Liberal M.P. for the city, announced that he would not be contesting the seat at the next election, and the president of the Trades Council then stated that 'certain gentlemen' had offered to contribute towards a fund for the return of a Labour candidate for Aberdeen. The Council decided that it was 'an inopportune time to press the return of such a candidate. The Council, however, should keep the matter in view for a future occasion.'[3]

The mid-'eighties were important formative years in the development of the Trades Council's policy of Labour representation. The first important move was made in 1884, when the Council nominated two of its members, G. Maconnochie, a printer, and J. Forbes, a shoemaker, as 'Labour' candidates in the municipal elections. Curiously enough, the initial impetus for this move derived from a seemingly unimportant

[1] *Daily Free Press*, 13 Mar. 1882.
[2] *Minutes*, 1 Mar. 1882; 11 Mar. 1882; 29 Mar. 1882. The Rev. C. C. Macdonald, a Radical and one of the Trades Council's nominees, himself 'thought that an effort should be made by the working-classes to return representatives of their own order to the School Board' (*Minutes*, 11 Mar. 1882).
[3] *Ibid.* 21 May 1884; *Daily Free Press*, 22 May 1884. The 'certain gentlemen' are unknown: possibly some of J. C. Thompson's Radical friends.

9 *

matter. Time after time in the 'eighties, the Trades Council expressed bitter opposition to proposals to increase the salaries of high-ranking officials of local public boards—such officials as the manager of the gasworks, the town clerk and city chamberlain, and the clerk and treasurer of the School Board. At bottom, this opposition was a reflection of class-feeling; it sprang from the thought that, although working-men were ignored, men of another class, already in comfortable circumstances, were being made still more comfortable. Thus, the Trades Council objected to proposals for the superannuation of parochial inspectors: 'They should be left to make provision for old age from their own savings the same as other members of the community.'[1] In 1884, the Town Council was considering increasing the salary of the superintendent of police; the Trades Council reacted strongly, and gained considerable public support for its stand at meetings of ratepayers. The question seems to have been the main immediate one on which the municipal election of that year turned.[2]

The two Trades Council candidates, apart from their attitude on this question—in which they were not alone—had little by way of a concrete programme, but their election speeches revealed a deeper note of discontent. Maconnochie 'charged the professed Liberals of the city in high stations with belying their creed when they went in opposition to his return. . . . These were the men who patted the working-classes on the back, but gave them nothing, and what they were afraid of was, not the return of the two Labour candidates at the present time, but that this would only be letting in the thin end of the wedge, and that by and by more Labour representatives would be returned. His contention was that the working-classes were entitled to a fair representation—he did not ask for more. . . .'[3] On this occasion, the thin end of the wedge was driven home: Forbes and Maconnochie

---

[1] *Minutes*, 13 April 1881. This sort of feeling is, of course, of considerable importance in nationalised industries today.

[2] *Ibid.* 27 Feb. 1884; 12 Mar. 1884; 24 Sep. 1884; 15 Oct. 1884.

[3] *Daily Free Press*, 4 Nov. 1884.

were both elected to the Town Council.[1] The result led to
the production of an unintentionally amusing collection of
rhymes, the anonymous work of someone who detested the
defeat of old and tried councillors by those who objected to
an increase in 'a bobby's pay':

'The rags and tatters of the town
Have pulled the flag of Merit down,
And thrown its ancient fair renown
    Behind an ugly cloud;
And made all cheap the civic crown
    Among the motley crowd.

'The people brook not autocrats,
But surely they have turned flats,
To choose a chieftain of cats
    To tested men and true;
But surely now the slumocrats
    Have had their day and due.

' "The little rift within the lute"
Will make the civic honour mute,
For this dark speck upon the fruit
    Shall soon corrupt the whole,
For what unknown degraded loot
    May not now go to poll?

'The crowd have now had length of rope,
The scum has risen to the top,
And given the death-blow to all hope
    Of civic fair repute;
The bloom prefigures a poor crop
    If this be Franchise fruit.'[2]

[1] 'It is gratifying to have to record the return of two Labour candidates
to the Town Council at the last election, which thus places Aberdeen in front
of any other town in Scotland as regards the furtherance of this important
movement' (*Report* of Aberdeen Trades Council for *1884*, quoted in W.
Diack, *op. cit.* p. 83).
[2] Anon. *Town Talk on the Municipal Election of November, 1884* (Pamphlet,
Aberdeen, 1884; in King's College Library, Aberdeen).

Heartened by this success, the 'slumocrats' of the Trades Council a few months later decided to take action in the approaching elections to the School Board. As a preliminary, an appeal to working-men was drafted and approved—an appeal which stated clearly the general position of the Trades Council on the question of labour representation:

'Fellow-workmen—It is the opinion of this Council that the time has arrived when they ought to take a fair share in the administration of our public Boards. . . . in the past the interests of labour have been neglected, and it cannot be otherwise as long as we continue to send to our public Boards men whose social position and interests differ so widely from the large majority of the working classes. . . . We must send to our Boards men of our own order who understand our position, who have interests in common with ourselves. . . . With this object in view, the Council appeal to you for funds. . . .'[1]

The Council nominated six candidates for the School Board elections; only two of them, however—J. Annand and J. C. Thompson—were workers. A conference was held with the clerical parties in an endeavour to effect a compromise and thereby avoid the necessity of recourse to the ballot-box; the clerical element was willing to agree to four Trades Council candidates, but the conference broke down over the insistence of the Trades Council on retaining all six of its candidates. Thus, for the first time for a number of years, ordinary voters in Aberdeen were given the opportunity of expressing an opinion on the conduct and membership of the School Board. The result of the poll was that all the Trades Council's candidates were among the fifteen elected.[2]

In that same year, 1885, there was a parliamentary

---

[1] *Daily Free Press*, 12 Feb. 1885.

[2] *Ibid.* 18 April 1885; *Minutes*, 11 Feb. 1885; 7 April 1885. The Radical Association supported the Trades Council candidates. Although the Council's success was a remarkable achievement, it should be remembered that a cumulative vote was allowed in School Board elections: a voter could, if he wished, give all fifteen of his votes to one candidate. Consequently, School Board elections were very uncertain affairs, as the Trades Council later discovered to its cost.

election: the first occasion on which, with an enlarged electorate,[1] there were to be two constituencies in Aberdeen. The sitting Liberal M.P. was retiring, and the Liberals of the city were therefore faced with the task of adopting two candidates. There was no difficulty over the adoption of J. Bryce as candidate for South Aberdeen, but the candidature for North Aberdeen was a different matter: it was there that the bulk of the working-class population of the town lived, and working-class Radicals were determined to exercise an effective voice in the choosing of a candidate. The Trades Council considered the possibility of bringing forward a working-man as a candidate, but was unable to meet the difficulty of supporting such a person financially if he were elected;[2] it was therefore decided, on the suggestion of the Radical Association, that the choosing of a Liberal candidate should be the responsibility of a conference of representatives of the Council and of the Liberal, Radical and Land-law Reform Associations. The Council of the Liberal Association met on 1 June and although no decision was taken as to a candidate, the leaders of the Association made it unmistakably clear that they had no intention of allowing the other three organisations to share in the choice of a candidate: the choice was to be that of the Liberal Association, which would welcome co-operation in securing the return of the chosen person.[3]

Thus, hostility between the Trades Council and the local caucus again came into the open, and resentment of the attitude of the Liberal leaders was a thread running through all speeches made at a special meeting of the Trades Council on 3 June. A. Catto struck the key-note when he referred to 'the very disrespectful way in which the Liberal Association

---

[1] The third Reform Act extended the franchise in the towns, besides enfranchising ratepayers in the counties.

[2] As an answer to this problem, G. Bisset suggested Broadhurst's name (Broadhurst, if elected, would not need to be paid by Aberdeen). In fact, Bisset put the suggestion to Broadhurst, but the latter had already decided to stand for another constituency (*Daily Free Press*, 7 May 1885; 21 May 1885).

[3] *Ibid.* 2 June 1885; *Minutes*, 6 May 1885; 13 June 1885.

treated our correspondence . . . and the contemptuous way in which they treated us as a Council and the representatives of the Council who were present at their last meeting. . . . we have arrived at that period in our history as working-men when we must look to ourselves to get men to represent ourselves (applause). It seems to me that the shop-keeping element and the upper class element in the Liberal Association are wanting to put us out of sight.' G. Bisset brought up a grievance of some standing when he reminded delegates that in the past no working-man had been elected as an official of the Liberal Association because, he alleged, such a proposal was distasteful to a section of the Liberals; and both Bisset and Mackintosh, themselves members of the executive committee of the Liberal Association, declared that if the Trades Council was now to act independently of the Association, they must sever their connection with one organisation or the other—and they would remain with the Council.[1] The Council then decided to invite W. Hunter, a Radical with advanced views on educational and land matters, to contest North Aberdeen 'in the interests of the working classes'.

A few days later, the Aberdeen Radical Association, which had for some time nursed Hunter as a prospective candidate, also extended an invitation to him. The Council of the Liberal Association, when it met on 8 June, followed suit, though not without such comments as those of one of its members, Simpson: 'The Trades Council had simply done them a very dirty trick. They had behaved like a great number of bad boys that had been spoiled by getting too much of their own way. . . .'[2] Hunter himself was careful to pay due respect to the Liberal Association, and, along with Bryce, was elected to represent Aberdeen in Parliament.

The incident did not then lead to any break between the Trades Council and the Liberal Association: Bisset, Catto,

[1] *Daily Free Press*, 4 June 1885. Mackintosh had some reservations about independent action: he thought it possible that the Conservatives might win the seat on a split vote, but this possibility seems to have been generally scouted on the ground of the weakness of the Conservative party in Aberdeen.
[2] *Ibid.* 9 June 1885.

and others of their persuasion continued to be active members of the Association, and in the general election of 1886 the Trades Council unanimously expressed continued confidence in Hunter and Bryce.[1] Yet it is difficult to avoid the conclusion that the breach which occurred a few years later might have been postponed a little had the Liberal caucus been more diplomatic and less condescending in its relations with trade unionists, had it been less inclined to treat them as boys, good or bad.

In the later years of the 'eighties, the Trades Council continued to take an interest in local government elections, but there was a visible slackening of the pressure for labour representation. To a considerable extent, this was due to the difficulty of finding working-men who, if elected, would be able to attend meetings of such bodies as the Town Council during the day-time. Maconnochie, who was elected to the Town Council in 1884, was able—with considerable self-sacrifice—to carry out his duties, since he was a night-worker; his companion, Forbes, was at first paid by the Trades Council for loss of wages (as were Trades Council representatives on the management boards of the Public Library and the Infirmary), but resigned from the Town Council in 1886. Occasionally a working-class candidate was nominated—J. C. Thompson stood for the Town Council in 1885 and 1887 and was defeated on both occasions, though Maconnochie was re-elected in the latter year; but in the main the Trades Council pursued a policy of backing any candidate, already nominated, who promised to support a particular aspect of Trades Council policy. In 1887, this particular aspect was temperance, and the Council entered into a short-lived alliance with a number of temperance bodies;[2] as a rule, however, the main concern of the Council

---

[1] *Minutes*, 26 June 1886. Hunter and Bryce were re-elected unopposed—a measure of Liberal strength in Aberdeen.

[2] *Ibid.* 12 Oct. 1887. The Trades Council was strongly teetotal. A minute of arrangements for a members' social evening reads: 'No spirituous liquors to be allowed. A good deal of discussion took place as to whether a bottle of wine should be got for the singers. . . .' The singers did get their bottle—after a good deal of discussion (*Minutes*, 28 Nov. 1888).

in municipal elections was to press for Town Council meetings to be held in the evenings so that working-men might stand for election.

The Trades Council was more active when the time came, in 1888, for the triennial School Board elections. It nominated six candidates, three of whom—J. Annand, W. Livingston, and J. C. Thompson—were working-men. As in 1885, the Council refused to compromise over the number of its candidates, but in the result only three (including Thompson) of the six were elected. Members of the Council referred to the apathy of the electorate and the hostility of the press, and condemned the cumulative voting system, but the result was recognised as a defeat.[1]

Nevertheless, if the Trades Council was less successful and less active in local elections in the late 'eighties, significant political developments were taking place amongst its members: it was in these years that the decisive break with Liberalism was being engineered. Until about 1885, the working-class rumblings of discontent, which were reflected, probably in a heightened form, in the Aberdeen Trades Council, could be construed simply as advanced Radicalism: the Council felt that it and the working-men it represented were entitled to a share in the direct administration of public affairs, and it wanted that administration to be more concerned with the needs of workers. But these changes could, it thought, be brought about within the Liberal party. The two main leaders of the movement, J. C. Thompson and G. Bisset, who were respectively presidents of the Council in 1883-5 and 1886-8, were Radicals: Thompson was a prime mover in the Aberdeen Radical Association, and Bisset explicitly described himself as 'an extreme Radical' in 1885.[2] In the next few years, however, many workers realised that the changes they envisaged could not be encompassed within the Liberal party, and

---

[1] Though the glee of the *Daily Free Press* was hardly justified: 'The result . . . is wholesome, and, in the main, highly satisfactory . . . this party has suffered complete and ignominious collapse' (*Daily Free Press*, 21 April 1888).

[2] *Ibid.* 12 Feb. 1885.

that what was required was a new and independent party; the realisation dawned slowly at first, and then with startling rapidity about 1890.

One indication of the way the wind was blowing came late in 1886. At the T.U.C. conference of that year, a Labour Electoral Committee—soon to be better known as the Labour Electoral Association—was set up, and Thompson, who had attended the conference, was prompted on his return to Aberdeen to propose that the Council add the words 'and Labour Electoral Association' to its name. Since the Council was already performing the functions suggested by the proposed change, this would have been merely formal, and the proposal was not adopted. Instead, the Council instructed its executive committee to 'consider what steps may be taken for the organisation of a strictly working class Political Association to secure more direct representation in Parliament and at our public boards. . . .'[1] Here was the germ of the idea of a third party, but the executive committee, having considered the matter, recommended caution: the question of cost was an important consideration to be borne in mind, and there were already a number of political associations in the city. Bisset, reporting for the executive, said that 'they thought unless there was a strong demand for such an association by the working classes, it would be better that at the present time, at least, the matter should not be gone on with. The object of the association, although political, was not a party one. It was to secure the interests of labour without attaching themselves to any party whatever.'[2] The Council therefore decided to ascertain the considered views of the various trade union branches, but the replies it received to a circular letter merely confirmed the general impression of uncertainty and flux in political ideas: the general burden of the replies was that the Council's suggestions in relation to the proposed political association were too vague. This was not very helpful, and the Council quietly shelved the proposal for the time being.[3]

[1] *Minutes*, 13 Oct. 1886.   [2] *Daily Free Press*, 11 Nov. 1886.
[3] *Minutes*, 3 Nov. 1886; 8 Dec. 1886; 19 Jan. 1887; 16 Feb. 1887.

Similarly, there was an indication of confusion and lack of grasp of political reality in 1887, when the Council was invited to affiliate to the Labour Electoral Association. The invitation was declined. 'The President explained that they had already declared for Home Rule for Scotland; and as then all questions that would be of special interest to Labour organisations would be under the Scottish Legislative Assembly, the Executive were of opinion that such a national association was unnecessary.'[1] Perhaps so—but the immediate reality was a parliament in Westminster, not Edinburgh.

Clarity was gained in the decisive debates in the Trades Council in the late 'eighties on the question of a statutory eight-hour working day. The acceptance of this by the Council as a desirable reform has been traced in an earlier chapter. Once accepted, the question immediately arose as to whether the Liberal party would be willing to sponsor it; and, if not, whether the formation of an independent Labour party would be necessary. However, to reach a full understanding of the significance of these questions in Aberdeen some reference to the role of H. H. Champion in national politics is required.

By the late 'eighties, H. H. Champion was one of the leading Socialist and Labour figures, in spite of the fact that his social background and habits were against him—he was an ex-army officer and he came from a landed family.[2] He was then perhaps the most prominent of the group of men, including Tom Mann and Keir Hardie, who aimed at the formation of a Labour party independent of both Liberals and Conservatives. His journal, *The Labour Elector*, which he published for two or three years from 1888, was probably the most influential of contemporary Labour newspapers; in it, besides attacking the connections between such trade union leaders as Broadhurst and big business men, he hammered

---

[1] *Minutes*, 12 Oct. 1887.

[2] The Urquhart family of Aberdeenshire. On his mother's side, Champion was the son of an Urquhart of Meldrum; on his father's side, a grandson of an Urquhart of Craigston (*Daily Free Press*, 22 June 1891). Champion's father was a major-general in the army.

home the need for a statutory eight-hour day, linking this with the prospect of forming an independent Labour party which would soon be able to hold the balance between the Liberal and Conservative parties as Parnell's Irish Nationalist party had done—no doubt Champion cast himself for the role of Parnell. More clearly than most Socialists, Champion saw the importance of the demand for a legal eight-hour day, and by 1889 *The Labour Elector* was well-known in trade union circles; it was, for example, virtually the organ of the London dockers during their great strike of that year. A. Catto, the Aberdeen bakers' union leader, later referred to the influence *The Labour Elector* had had on him—he was a regular subscriber to it in the late 'eighties.[1]

Champion's first political appearance in Aberdeen seems to have been made in 1887 or 1888, when he undertook a lecture tour under the auspices of the Scottish Land and Labour League and the Scottish Socialist Federation. Aberdeen was one of the towns he visited, and while there he made the acquaintance of G. Bisset, G. Gerrie, and several other left-wing Liberals. He did not return to the city until 1890, but in the interval he kept up correspondence with the friends he had made there.[2] In effect, these friends, of whom the most important was Gerrie, comprised most of the leadership of the Aberdeen Junior Liberal Association. They seem to have been deeply impressed by Champion and his ideas, and it was probably no accident that about this time, in 1888, when the Junior Liberal Association became defunct, Gerrie 'gathered round him a little band of personal friends who subsequently formed themselves into the "Aberdeen Labour Committee" '.[3]

It is not difficult to see the indirect influence of Champion or *The Labour Elector* in the debates on an eight-hour day which took place in the Aberdeen Trades Council in 1888-9. On one occasion the Council, on Bisset's motion, explicitly declared its support for Champion in the exposure currently being made by *The Labour Elector* of bad conditions suffered

[1] *Daily Free Press*, 3 Mar. 1892.   [2] *Ibid.* 15 June 1891; 8 May 1893.
[3] W. Diack, *op. cit.* p. 22.

by workers employed by Brunner, Mond and Co., a chemical firm with which Broadhurst had some connections.[1] And the progress of Bisset and Catto towards the standpoint of independent Labour representation was marked by their appearance as two of the four main speakers at an evening meeting held in Dundee concurrently with the T.U.C. conference there in 1889: the meeting adopted resolutions in favour of the formation of a new Labour parliamentary party to secure a legal eight-hour day.[2]

A month later, Bisset and his friends made an unsuccessful attempt to secure Liberal endorsement of the eight-hour day movement. Bisset, Catto, Beveridge, Gerrie, and W. C. Spence were amongst those present at a conference in Aberdeen of delegates from Liberal Associations in the north-east of Scotland, and Bisset proposed that no government employee should be required to work longer than eight hours a day nor should he receive less than the standard rate of wages. Most of the delegates present evidently considered this an embarrassing proposal: the chairman attempted unsuccessfully to prevent discussion of it, and the previous question was moved. Bisset replied with a veiled threat by saying that he and his friends 'wished to keep up the connection that had hitherto existed between the Liberal party and the working class, but if they were to be treated with scorn, as on that occasion, by some persons in the Liberal party . . . and proposals were to be met with the previous question so that there might be no discussion, they would know at what expense they were to receive their support and whether they were prepared to pay the price for it'.[3] But the previous question was carried by a vote of thirty against twenty.

In effect, what was happening in Aberdeen was the grafting of the concrete issue of the eight-hour day on to the

[1] *Minutes*, 29 May 1889.
[2] *Daily Free Press*, 4 Sep. 1889. Cunninghame Graham and Edward Aveling were the other two main speakers at the meeting. Catto was not attending the T.U.C. on behalf of the Aberdeen Trades Council; he was probably representing the Scottish Operative Bakers' Federal Union.
[3] *Ibid.* 23 Oct. 1889.

WILLIAM DIACK (*c.* 1939)

dissatisfaction, already prevalent but vague in expression, with the Liberal party. Champion addressed the big May Day demonstration in 1890, and his twin emphasis on the eight-hour day and independent Labour representation made a profound impression on his audience: indeed, the Trades Council decided to print 5,000 copies of his speech for sale at 1d. each.[1] In the evening, after the demonstration, Champion further expounded his views to a select meeting composed mainly of members of the Trades Council and such dissident Liberals as Bisset and Gerrie. 'The discussion resolved itself into a triangular duel between the respective merits of the Trades Council, the Liberal Association, or a distinct labour organisation as the most effective means of carrying out their programme'[2]—the programme consisting largely of a statutory eight-hour day. Apparently, it was decided not to form a new political organisation but to leave the agitation for an eight-hour day in the competent hands of the Trades Council; however, a Labour Committee was established as an independent body. The Aberdeen Labour Committee was, in fact, simply the group established informally by Gerrie in 1888: it was composed solely of middle-class and professional men such as Gerrie, Beveridge, Spence, and Bisset (who was now an employer), who were ineligible for membership of trade unions, and therefore of the Trades Council. The Labour Committee—a misnomer, since its members represented only themselves—conceived its function to be 'to provide for those who were willing to assist the [Trades] Council on any labour questions of importance', and the Council heartily agreed to accept this offer of co-operation.[3]

Another outcome of Champion's visit was the unanimous resolve 'That the members of the Trades Council pledge themselves to make the interest of labour the first and determining question in all their political action imperial and local'.[4] This expression of principle was moved by

[1] *Minutes*, 28 May 1890.   [2] *Daily Free Press*, 19 May 1890.
[3] *Minutes*, 4 June 1890; 9 July 1890; 2 Oct. 1890.
[4] *Ibid.* 2 July 1890.

10

J. Keir, vice-president of the Council and a supporter of Champion, whose meaning was made plain in his speech: 'Although the Council had on many occasions acted independently of any party in consideration of labour questions, he thought it would be generally admitted that they were as a rule looked upon as belonging to the Liberal or Radical party. He thought in supporting that party they had not on all occasions done the very best things possible for the interests of labour . . . they found very often that men, who were going on their Radical platforms and delivering most advanced speeches, exercised in their own works a very different spirit towards their employees. . . .'[1] And Keir was careful to emphasise the fact that he was not a Tory.

The Trades Council incorporated the demand for an eight-hour day (for employees of the Town Council) in its municipal election programme of 1890,[2] and for several years after that the question was virtually the touchstone of the independent Labour movement in the city. Liberal leaders who found the demand inconvenient were constantly harassed by attempts to pin them down. Thus Bryce, Liberal M.P. for South Aberdeen, addressed a meeting held under the auspices of the Trades Council on 21 May 1891; he spoke at length on the eight-hours question, opposing a general Bill but suggesting experiments in various industries.[3] A few days later, on 25 May, the *Daily Free Press* commented editorially: 'The legislative eight hours all round is an awkward question for the political trimmer. . . . This is one of the questions on which the split is taking place between the "Labour" party and the "popular" politicians . . . the "popular" politician is coming to be more and more distrusted by those to whom he addresses his plausible speeches.'

The eight-hour day became almost an obsession with Champion and constant reiteration of the theme—it was

---

[1] *Daily Free Press*, 3 July 1890. Another speaker in the debate on the motion made it clear that it derived from Champion's meeting.

[2] *Minutes*, 10 Oct. 1890. No candidates were directly nominated by the Trades Council, though Maconnochie was again re-elected.

[3] *Daily Free Press*, 22 May 1891. In Leatham's opinion, Bryce was 'an able but barren balancer' (J. Leatham, *loc. cit.* vol. XXIX, no. 341, p. 18).

the basis of his election campaign in Aberdeen in 1892—
certainly gained him considerable support. It seems possible,
however, that Champion over-played his hand on this
point: he was not content to advocate an eight-hour day as
a useful reform, but implied that it would be the solution of
the problem of unemployment. Consequently, his journal,
the *Aberdeen Labour Elector*, was at pains to attempt to counter-
act the publicity given to an experiment conducted by
Allan, a Sunderland engineering employer, in 1893.[1] Allan
introduced the eight-hour day into his works, and claimed
that as a result he got more work done per man owing to
greater continuity of work. In effect, this knocked the bottom
out of Champion's argument on unemployment, and the
Aberdeen Labour Elector betrayed anxiety in asserting that
Allan had not really reduced the number of hours worked
by his men: all he had done was to 're-arrange' the hours
so as to eliminate sleeping and slacking at work. It was an
ingenious but not very convincing refutation of Allan's
claims.

[1] *Aberdeen Labour Elector*, 18 May 1893.

CHAPTER X

TRADES COUNCIL AND INDEPENDENT LABOUR

In February 1891, a conference of representatives of the
Trades Council and the Aberdeen Labour Committee met
to discuss political matters and recommended the Council to
convene a meeting of delegates from all Trades Councils in
Scotland 'for the purpose of securing united action in
pressing forward measures for bettering the condition of the
working class'; it was suggested that the agenda of such a
meeting should include consideration of means of securing
the return of a body of Labour M.P.s for Scotland, payment
of M.P.s, a statutory eight-hour day, and abolition of the
conspiracy laws.[1] With P. Milne as the only dissentient, the
Trades Council adopted this recommendation, and the
secretary was instructed to sound out the opinion of other
Trades Councils. The response was encouraging, and
arrangements were made for the meeting; on the score of
expense of travel, however, it was decided to hold it in a
more central place than Aberdeen, and the Edinburgh
Trades Council agreed to act as host, general convening
arrangements remaining in the hands of Aberdeen. Keir
Hardie showed interest in the proposed conference, and at
his suggestion it was agreed that it should not be confined
to trade unionists: any association might send delegates
provided that it secured credentials from the Trades Council
in its area.[2]

The conference took place in Edinburgh on 8 August
1891, and was more successful than its promoters had dared
to hope. Besides a few representatives of Labour political
organisations, such as the Dumfries Labour party, and a few

[1] *Minutes,* 25 Feb. 1891.
[2] *Ibid.* 4 Mar. 1891; 28 April 1891; 27 May 1891; 1 July 1891; *Daily
Free Press,* 11 June 1891. Hardie was concerned to prevent the exclusion of
such men as Cunninghame Graham and H. H. Champion.

prominent men such as Keir Hardie, the conference was made up of delegates from most of the Scottish Trades Councils: in all, there were sixty-seven people present, representing organisations with a membership of eighty-four thousand. W. Johnston, one of the delegates from the Aberdeen Trades Council,[1] modestly explained that the object of the conveners was 'to pave the way for holding, perhaps, an annual conference of representatives of all trades in the country', but the meeting, in its resolutions, went beyond this. The main resolution set the key-note: 'This conference, recognising the need for direct representation of labour in Parliament and on local administrative boards, recommends that wherever a candidate is put forward by recognised local labour organisations, and whose candidature is in no wise connected with either great political parties, every possible effort should be made by the trade organisations of this country to assist him financially and otherwise.'[2] Resolutions were also carried in favour of a statutory eight-hour day and the payment of M.P.s by the State. A further conference was to be held in Glasgow at a later date, and meanwhile an executive committee was to be established, consisting of one representative from each of the Trades Councils in Scotland.

The significance of the conference was that for the first time a large number of Scottish trade unionists were being directly associated with a policy of independent Labour representation. Keir Hardie's view of the importance of this step was expressed when he addressed the Aberdeen Trades Council two months later. He complimented the Council on its advanced political attitude and for having promoted the Edinburgh conference which, in Hardie's opinion, 'had given an impetus to the forward movement in this country, which in his most sanguine expectations of less than a year ago, he did not hope for within the next 20 years. They

---

[1] One of the other two Aberdeen delegates, W. S. Rennie, was a member of the Aberdeen Socialist Society, which approved of the conference (see *The Workers' Herald*, 26 Dec. 1891; 9 Jan. 1892).

[2] *Daily Free Press*, 10 Aug. 1891.

10 *

had no possible conception of the influence that that conference had had amongst their fellow working-men in the
south, east, and west of Scotland. Previous to that conference
the idea of a Labour party was supposed to be the product
of irresponsible individuals, like himself, for example, but
since the Edinburgh Conference, the ordinary working-man
. . . had got the idea into his brain that the leaders of
labour in Scotland saw the necessity for and the urgent need
for labour political unions in Scotland as they had labour
trade unions.'[1] Hardie clearly saw the new organisation as a
valuable adjunct to the Scottish Labour party.

When the second conference was held in Glasgow on 5
March 1892, the Scottish United Trades Councils' Labour
party was formally established. The name was apt: the
interim executive committee, now confirmed in office,
consisted of representatives of the Trades Councils of Glasgow, Edinburgh, Aberdeen, Arbroath, Dunfermline, Falkirk,
Govan, Kilmarnock, Kirkcaldy, and Paisley,[2] together with
Carson, representing the Scottish Labour party. G. Bisset,
who apparently represented the Aberdeen Labour Committee, thought he was perhaps the only person present at
the conference who was not a representative of a Trades
Council. The conference adopted a lengthy programme of
urgently needed reforms, headed by the legal eight-hour day
and including the nationalisation of the land, mines, and
railways, and suggested that branches of the new party
should be organised by Trades Councils: 'We recommend
that the Trades Councils in their respective centres should
be the responsible recognised managers of the branches of
the proposed labour representation party, that the Trades
Councils be looked upon as the head of the branches in the

[1] *Daily Free Press*, 1 Oct. 1891. Possibly Hardie, in deference to his hosts,
was expressing his views in an exaggerated fashion.

[2] In addition, the Trades Council of Motherwell was part of the movement,
and that of Montrose was probably so. The Trades Councils of Dundee,
Greenock and Port Glasgow remained aloof, presumably because of Liberal
influence in them (though the Dundee Trades Council had attended the
Edinburgh conference, and had two nominees on the Dundee Town Council
in 1890).

centre in which each exists, and no branch shall be recognised in any centre unless it has the approval of the Trades Council in that centre, if such Trades Council be affiliated with the Trades Council Labour Party.'[1]

A month later, the Aberdeen Trades Council decided to call a public meeting, with the co-operation of the Labour Committee, to set up a branch of the Scottish United Trades Councils' Labour party. The meeting was held on 20 May 1892, with R. C. Robertson, secretary of the party and a miners' leader, as the main speaker, and a branch was duly formed in Aberdeen—whereupon the Aberdeen Labour Committee went out of existence.[2] One interesting point arose at this public meeting when Robertson was asked by a Liberal in the audience whether a member of the Liberal Association would be eligible for membership of the new party: Robertson replied, 'Certainly.'[3]

Meanwhile, during the previous year, important developments had taken place in Aberdeen. From May 1891, the Aberdeen Labour Committee was busy covertly canvassing the name of H. H. Champion as a possible Labour candidate for the parliamentary constituency of South Aberdeen. Although Champion addressed several meetings in the city in 1891, his supporters were cautious and made no definite proposals in public that he should be adopted. There were difficulties to be surmounted. Some of them centred on the personality and reputation of Champion himself. He was inclined to be tactless, and his manner aroused distrust in the minds of some workers. Thus, to Leatham, 'he was handsome and clever and well-intentioned; but he came among us with the air of making a sacrifice and doing a great favour'.[4] When Champion severely criticised J. Havelock Wilson, the national secretary of the seamen's union, for alleged mishandling of the union's affairs, J. C. Thompson,

[1] Report of the executive committee (as amended and adopted), given in *Daily Free Press*, 7 Mar. 1892.

[2] *Minutes*, 13 April 1892; 3 May 1892; 25 May 1892.

[3] *Daily Free Press*, 21 May 1892. It is uncertain whether officials of the Liberal Association would have been barred from membership.

[4] J. Leatham, *loc. cit.* vol. XXIX, no. 341, p. 18.

the union's secretary in Aberdeen, was alienated: in fact, Thompson became one of the most bitter critics of Champion, and abruptly reversed his previous movement away from the Liberal party.[1] Champion's reputation was by no means so high as it had been two years before; in fact, it had been irretrievably damned in the eyes of most British workers by his intervention in the big Australian strike in 1890. Champion was in Australia at the time, and formed the opinion that the strike was a mistake and was bound to fail; he therefore cabled John Burns, urging that contributions should not be sent by British working-class organisations to the Australian strikers. He may or may not have been right in his view of the strike: what was apparent, both to British and Australian workers, was that this action was a poor return for the £30,000 which had been sent by Australians to the London dock strikers a few months before. Probably only in Newcastle and Aberdeen did Champion, on his return from Australia, regain a good deal of his lost reputation, and he depended much on the devotion of the Aberdeen Labour Committee—he was able to inspire loyalty as well as distrust. But even in Aberdeen his popularity had suffered by 1891.[2]

There were other reasons for being cautious about putting forward an independent Labour parliamentary candidate. As far as the middle-class members of the Labour Committee were concerned, the die was cast with the calling of the Edinburgh conference of Trades Councils in 1891: Gerrie's group now stood openly and unequivocally for a policy of independent Labour representation, and there was no going back on it. G. Bisset resigned his position as a vice-president of the Liberal Association of North Aberdeen in June, and severed his connections with Liberalism.[3] On the face of it, the Aberdeen Trades Council was equally committed to an independent Labour policy. But the members of the Council did not find it easy to break completely their old association with the Liberal party, in spite

[1] *Daily Free Press*, 20 June 1891.   [2] *Minutes*, 4 Mar. 1891; 24 June 1891.
[3] *Daily Free Press*, 23 June 1891.

of the formation of the Scottish United Trades Councils' Labour party. The municipal elections of 1891 provided the occasion both for what was to be—with one temporary exception in 1900—the last show of willingness by the Council as a whole to co-operate with the Liberal party, and for the final break with that party.

It was an open secret that the Trades Council envisaged putting forward two Labour candidates—W. Johnston and G. Bisset—in the municipal elections of 1891, but before definitely deciding on this step the Council appointed a committee to confer with the officials of the various trade unions in Aberdeen. The conference was held on 23 September, and was immediately thrown into confusion by a letter from the Liberal Association. The latter body had decided, for the first time for a number of years, to take part in the municipal elections: it asked for the co-operation of the Trades Council and certain other bodies (mainly temperance organisations) in deciding upon a programme and candidates for the elections. The conference of trade unionists, after some hesitation, agreed to send representatives to a joint meeting at the offices of the Liberal Association, and these representatives were instructed to put forward a model election programme issued by the Glasgow Trades Council. This was done, and the meeting convened by the Liberals accepted the Trades Council programme with only slight amendments; it was further agreed to call ward meetings of voters to select candidates who would support this programme.[1]

Consequently, when the Trades Council met on 30 September, it considered a recommendation by its *ad hoc* committee to co-operate with the Liberal Association and other bodies. A number of leaders of the Council disliked the recommendation: T. Nicol, the president, 'protested as much

---

[1] *Minutes*, 16 Sep. 1891; 23 Sep. 1891; *Daily Free Press*, 22 Sep. 1891; 24 Sep. 1891; 26 Sep. 1891. The main points of the election programme of the Glasgow Trades Council were: municipalisation of tramways, public control of the liquor traffic, taxation of land values, the 'fair wages' clause in municipal contracts, building of artisans' dwellings, and evening Town Council meetings.

as he could against having anything to do with the Liberal Association'; A. Catto wanted the Council to nominate two Labour candidates, 'and let the Liberal Association support them if they cared'. But J. C. Thompson supported the recommendation, and R. Boice 'counselled the Committee to work in harmony with' and not in defiance of the Liberal Association. This latter viewpoint was that of most members of the Council, and the recommendation was accepted on a vote of twenty-five against thirteen.[1]

But although co-operation was thus decided upon, it proved an uneasy alliance. The temperance organisations declined to pay their share of the expenses of the proposed ward meetings; they and the Liberals were alleged to be selecting candidates privately without waiting for the ward meetings; and the Liberal Association was apparently manœuvring with a view to keeping the arrangements for these meetings in the hands of the officials of its ward organisations.[2] Considerable surprise and resentment was expressed by some groups of workers at the Trades Council's action in apparently not pressing the candidatures of Johnston and Bisset: for example, at a branch meeting of the shipwrights' society 'some very severe comments were passed upon the officials for having, as certain speakers described it, "betrayed the interests of labour in entering into a combination with the Liberal Association"'.[3] When the first of the ward meetings was held, Bisset was proposed as a candidate for the ward and so, in opposition to him, was Baillie Lyon, who was not present at the meeting. The discussion of the merits of the two men turned on their attitude to the agreed programme: Bisset accepted it, but Lyon's supporters, who were Liberals, made it clear that their nominee did not and that they did not suppose that any man could reasonably accept all the points in it.[4]

---

[1] *Minutes*, 30 Sep. 1891.   [2] *Ibid.* 5 Oct. 1891; 7 Oct. 1891.
[3] *Daily Free Press*, 9 Oct. 1891.
[4] *Ibid.* 14 Oct. 1891. At a voters' meeting in another ward three days later, the programme was discussed point by point and severely amended: the Liberal Association either could not or would not control its ward organisations.

That was the last straw as far as the Trades Council was concerned: it had agreed upon co-operation with the Liberal Association on the basis of a particular programme, but it was now clear that the Liberals looked on the programme as a ragbag collection of possible reforms, not as a set of firm promises. On 14 October, the Council reversed its decision to co-operate with the Liberal Association; the voting was thirty-four against five, a significant pointer to the feeling amongst Council members.[1] Two weeks later, the Council recommended five men, including Johnston, Bisset and Beveridge, as 'Labour candidates', and Johnston and Bisset were successful in the poll. This time the resentment at what was considered to be the trickery of the Liberal caucus did not fade into the background as in 1885. It remained, and one sign of it was noted by the *Daily Free Press* in its report of the annual meeting of the Aberdeen Liberal Association: 'The members of the Trades Council, it was noticed, were conspicuous by their almost entire absence.'[2]

During the next two or three years there was a curious political development in the Trades Council. On the one hand, the movement for independent Labour representation reached a high peak, and commanded a steady majority in the Council. On the other hand, there emerged a minority group of Liberal trade unionists, led by W. Livingston,[3] who were ready to fight out every political issue with the independent Labour supporters in the Council. This latter development was all the more surprising since nothing comparable had taken place in the years preceding 1892. There had been a struggle over the statutory eight-hour day, but it had been conducted on the merits of the proposal, and by May 1890 virtually all members of the Council supported it: Livingston himself had spoken in its favour from one of

---

[1] *Minutes*, 14 Oct. 1891. Nicol's opinion was that if the ward meeting which had already been held could be taken as a criterion of those that were to follow, 'the farce should end' (*Daily Free Press*, 15 Oct. 1891).

[2] *Ibid.* 15 Dec. 1891.

[3] A member of the Trades Council throughout the 'eighties and 'nineties; he was its president in 1889. Livingston was elected as vice-president of the North Aberdeen Liberal Association in March 1892.

the platforms at the May Day demonstration of that year. Again, there had been very little opposition in the Council to the formation of the Scottish Trades Councils' Labour party. There was some opposition to the proposal that a branch of the party be formed in Aberdeen, yet a week after it had actually been formed a motion was carried in the Trades Council—apparently without dissent—cordially approving the event.[1] This motion was moved by J. McHardy, of the associated joiners', and seconded by R. Boice, of the Scottish operative tailors'—men and union branches very soon to be identified with the Liberal standpoint. Livingston, according to a later report, was one of the first members of the Aberdeen branch of the Scottish Trades Councils' Labour party:[2] he joined at about the same time as he was beginning to wage war on the concept of independent Labour representation.

No doubt part of the apparent confusion and contradiction in the attitude of such men as Livingston, Hardy, and Boice may be explained by the fact that membership of the Scottish Trades Councils' Labour party was open to men who were still members of the Liberal Association: a Liberal trade unionist who was attracted by the idea of Labour representation, whether independent or not, could enjoy the luxury of joining the new party without cutting adrift from the old. A clear-cut decision might thereby be postponed a little. But such temporising was very short in duration, for there occurred a remarkably rapid hardening of opinion amongst local trade union leaders in 1892: those who had not hitherto made up their minds took decisions, one way or the other, which were permanent in most cases. As the Trades Council had already seemed to opt solidly for the independent Labour viewpoint, this hardening of opinion

---

[1] *Minutes*, 25 May 1892.

[2] *Aberdeen Labour Elector*, 11 Feb. 1893; 25 Feb. 1893. Livingston is also said to have joined the Fabian Society in 1892. There were vague references to the existence of a Fabian Society in Aberdeen (*Daily Free Press*, 31 Mar. 1892), but in the opinion of the *Aberdeen Labour Elector*, 18 Feb. 1893, 'the local labour men ought to be sincerely thankful that there are no Fabians in the city'.

made itself apparent mainly in the sudden crystallisation of a determined Liberal grouping in its midst. The precise reasons for this are not obvious. Probably the fact of the General Election in 1892 was largely instrumental. The election served as a forcing house: with an independent Labour candidate being proposed in South Aberdeen, it was no longer possible for individuals to sit on the fence. Opinions had to be declared on this concrete issue and, once declared, they were hardened and tempered in the heat of the election campaign.

It may be also that the Newcastle programme of the Liberal party made an important contribution to the decision of some trade union leaders—and no doubt a much larger number of ordinary trade unionists—in Aberdeen to discard their doubts and throw themselves wholeheartedly behind the Liberal party. The programme adopted by the party in conference at Newcastle in October 1891 consisted of a number of political reforms, headed by Home Rule; reforms in the land-laws; and (the part which particularly interested trade unionists) reform of the law relating to employers' liability for accidents; and vague references to limiting the hours of labour and to the payment of M.P.s. The promise of a new Employers' Liability Bill was important to trade unionists: over the previous decade, the Aberdeen Trades Council, through its Parliamentary Bills standing committee, had kept a very sharp watch on proposed amendments to the law on this subject, and had frequently urged local M.P.s to take action in the matter.[1] The reference to the hours of labour made no promise of an eight-hours Bill, as advocates of independent Labour were quick to point out, but at least it was a crumb of comfort. The Newcastle programme, then, may well have been just sufficient to convince many trade unionists whose loyalty to the Liberal party had been strained to remain within the party: many of them must have thought that there was, in any case, no prospect of a new party achieving power in the

[1] E.g. see *Minutes*, 26 Mar. 1879; 11 Jan. 1882; 27 July 1887; 23 May 1888.

immediate future. Certain it is that the new Liberal grouping in the Trades Council first gave battle to the independent Labour men, with the Newcastle programme as its banner.

On 30 March 1892, A. Catto proposed that the Trades Council invite H. H. Champion to 'meet the electors of South Aberdeen at an early date with the view of his being selected to contest the division in the interests of Labour'. In spite of opposition from J. C. Thompson and P. Milne, the motion was carried by a vote of thirty to twenty.[1] The next item of business at this meeting was a motion proposed by W. Livingston: 'That . . . this Council resolves in the interests of labour to do its utmost for the return of a strong majority of Members of Parliament pledged to support Mr. Gladstone in carrying out the Newcastle Programme.' Livingston stressed the need for cohesion in the Liberal party, and 'thought it was their duty to put forward as many men as possible who were favourable to the Newcastle programme and also with as little friction as could be, as many bona fide labour representatives as possible'. J. Keir and others opposed the motion, pointing out the difference between the Newcastle programme and that of the Scottish Trades Councils' Labour party, and when a vote was taken at the next meeting of the Council Livingston's motion was defeated by forty to seventeen.[2]

The issue was thus joined, and the first round had gone to the 'independents'. Champion nearly threw away his advantage by tactlessly asking for details of the vote of 30 March—the names of those who had voted for or against him, or abstained, together with their trades and the number of men they represented—so that he might judge whether it was worth his while to accept the invitation. It was too high-handed a way of dealing with such an independent body as the Aberdeen Trades Council, and Nicol, the president, spoke for the Council as a whole when he made

---

[1] *Minutes*, 30 Mar. 1892; 2 Mar. 1892. About twenty delegates abstained from voting (*Daily Free Press*, 28 April 1892): this is, incidentally, almost the sole occasion on which it is possible to gain any idea of the number of abstentions in a Trades Council vote.   [2] *Minutes*, 13 April 1892.

the sharp rejoinder that 'if Mr. Champion wanted to know the feeling of the electors of Aberdeen he must come to the city and see what support he would get'.[1] However, Champion decided to accept the invitation, and received the support of the Scottish Trades Councils' Labour party; and on 23 June 1892, on the eve of the election campaign, the Trades Council formally recommended to the electors Champion as an independent Labour candidate for the south division of the city, and Hunter, the sitting Liberal M.P., for the north division.[2] In a three-cornered struggle for the South Aberdeen seat, Bryce (Liberal) received 3,513 votes, McCullagh (Conservative) 1,768, and Champion 991: it was a disappointing result for Champion's supporters, but they had the consolation of knowing that their candidate's vote was the highest polled by independent Labour in Scotland. Possibly Champion would have done better to have chosen North Aberdeen, which was a much more strongly working-class constituency, but there the Liberal representative still retained the support of the great majority of trade unionists.

With the General Election over, it was soon apparent that the new Liberal grouping in the Council had constituted itself a permanent opposition. J. I. Mundie moved to instruct the delegate to the T.U.C. conference of 1892 to take appropriate action 'so that it may be made distinctly clear that all future action of the organised trades be made distinct from either political party': a division was forced on this motion, but it was carried by thirty-eight votes to sixteen.[3]

---

[1] *Minutes*, 27 April 1892; 11 May 1892. Catto took the same view as Nicol.

[2] *Ibid.* 23 June 1892; *Daily Free Press*, 31 May 1892. The Aberdeen Socialist Society—two or three of whose leaders were members of the committee of the Aberdeen branch of the Scottish Trades Councils' Labour party —also supported Champion, although it looked askance at his past record (*Daily Free Press*, 10 Aug. 1891; 1 Mar. 1892).

[3] *Minutes*, 18 Aug. 1892; 31 Aug. 1892. At the T.U.C., A. Catto, representing the Scottish bakers, moved an amendment to insert the word 'Independent' before 'Labour' in Keir Hardie's successful motion instructing the Parliamentary Committee to prepare a scheme for Labour representation: Catto's amendment was carried by 141 votes to 140 (*Daily Free Press*, 8 Sep. 1892).

At the same time, in August 1892, the Aberdeen branch of the Scottish Trades Councils' Labour party and the Aberdeen Socialist Society asked the Trades Council to appoint a committee to act jointly with them in the next municipal elections. Again the Council was divided: forty-one members favoured the suggestion, whilst twenty-five others preferred an amendment by Boice that the committee to be appointed should act 'with any other organised body having a similar object and desiring co-operation'.[1] J. C. Thompson supported Boice and went further: 'the two Associations from whom he had a mandate were not to be tied up to this independent Labour party whatever. These Associations were practically Liberal to the backbone. . . .'[2] This was followed up by a letter to the Council from the branches of both tailors' unions, declaring that the defeat of Boice's amendment was indicative of too narrow an outlook. Nicol, in the chair, countered immediately by saying that it was open to any body which wished to co-operate with the Council to express such a desire, as the two left-wing organisations had. A few weeks later there came another, less diplomatic, counter from the branch of the boot and shoe operatives' union, in the form of an intimation that it had 'almost unanimously' instructed its delegates to the Council to support independent political action.[3]

Meanwhile, the joint committee of the three organisations had met and had drawn up a detailed programme for the municipal elections. The principal item of the programme was that the Town Council should hold its meetings in the evenings or alternatively that its members should be paid for attendance at afternoon meetings. Candidates were chosen to contest seven wards: since the fact that meetings were held in the afternoons was the main barrier to working-men becoming members of the Town Council, the intention was—in the words of W. Cooper of the Aberdeen Socialist

---

[1] *Minutes*, 31 Aug. 1892.

[2] *Daily Free Press*, 1 Sep. 1892. Catto, in reply, doubted whether Thompson had a mandate on this question from either of the two unions he represented (the ironmoulders, and the seamen and firemen).

[3] *Minutes*, 14 Sep. 1892; 12 Oct. 1892.

Rev. ALEXANDER WEBSTER (*c.* 1901)

Society—to 'run a sufficient number of candidates to force this question down the throats of the Town Council'.[1] The intention was not carried out, however, as the Lord Provost, Stewart, was approached by a number of prominent personalities in the city with the request that he remain in office for a further term, and he agreed to do so on condition that there were no evening meetings of the Town Council. The manœuvre disheartened the five working-men who had been chosen as candidates, and they all withdrew their names, leaving only three middle-class nominees of the Scottish Trades Councils' Labour party. The Trades Council approved the candidature of these three men, and rejected a proposal, moved by Leys (a Conservative) and Boice (a Liberal), to withdraw from the joint committee: the Socialist Society, on the other hand, did withdraw, in disgust at the retreat from the original plan. All three Labour candidates—Beveridge, Glass, and Gray—were successful at the poll.[2]

Finding themselves permanently outnumbered, the Liberal members of the Trades Council tried different tactics. Thus Boice, on behalf of the tailors, argued that 'the fees payable to the Trades Council were for labour purposes only and not for the political purposes of a certain portion of the community':[3] the 'certain portion of the community' was the Scottish Trades Councils' Labour party. When the Trades Council agreed to co-operate with the Labour party in the May Day demonstration in favour of an eight-hour day, Livingston 'did not object to the demonstration but he objected to the funds of the Council being made available for such a purpose'.[4]

A more desperate move was the disaffiliation from the Trades Council of a number of union branches in January 1893. The number of unions which seceded at this time is not known: it certainly included the two with which J. C. Thompson was associated—the ironmoulders and the seamen

---

[1] *Daily Free Press*, 11 Oct. 1892; 19 Sep. 1892.

[2] *Minutes*, 28 Sep. 1892; 26 Oct. 1892. Maconnochie had left Aberdeen by this time.   [3] *Ibid.* 15 Feb. 1893.   [4] *Ibid.* 29 Mar. 1893.

11

—together with the boilermakers and the amalgamated joiners; it may also have included the associated joiners, the plumbers, and the engineers. The split was of very short duration in some cases. The ironmoulders re-affiliated to the Council in June 1893, and the amalgamated joiners were also back in the fold by September. Their return was due more to a desire not to be isolated from the mainstream of trade union activity than to any change of political viewpoint. The *Aberdeen Labour Elector* thought it significant that J. C. Thompson was not one of the four delegates sent to the Council by the ironmoulders' branch when it re-affiliated,[1] but a few weeks later, when the Council was considering co-operating again with the I.L.P. in municipal elections, one of the ironmoulders' delegates threatened that 'the moulders would withdraw their delegates if any connection were to subsist between the Trades Council and the Labour party'.[2] Nevertheless, the threat was not carried into effect although the Council did co-operate with the I.L.P. on this occasion.

Possibly the return of the ironmoulders' and the amalgamated joiners' delegates to the Council after so short an absence had been connected with the dissolution of the Scottish Trades Councils' Labour party. The party had gone some way towards establishing itself in 1892. Branches had early been established in Glasgow and Edinburgh,[3] and at the annual conference, held in Aberdeen on 25 March 1893, the executive committee claimed that the party had thirty branches. However, the position had been radically changed by the formation of the I.L.P. at a conference in Bradford in January of that year: here at last was a national organisation which showed promise of welding together all the independent Labour groupings which had sprung up in various parts of Britain. The executive committee of the Scottish Trades Councils' Labour party therefore recommended that the party be dissolved, since it was now 'a waste

[1] *Aberdeen Labour Elector*, 29 June 1893. From this time, J. C. Thompson ceased to figure in trade union affairs.   [2] *Minutes*, 19 July 1893.
[3] *Daily Free Press*, 16 May 1892; 30 June 1892.

of power', and that branches should join the I.L.P.[1] The
recommendation was a recognition of what in fact was
already happening—the attendance at this conference in
Aberdeen was poor—and it was accepted.

It was a decision which was well received by trade
unionists in Aberdeen. Liberals such as Livingston were glad
to see the disappearance of the direct link between the
Trades Council and what was now to be known as the
Aberdeen I.L.P.—although in practice the latter body had,
since its foundation the previous year, been independent and
without any integral connection with the Trades Council.
The independent Labour supporters, for their part, already
had their party organisation firmly established, and intended
to join the national I.L.P.: they had deputed H. H. Champion to represent them at the inaugural conference at
Bradford, but he had been too ill to attend. As it turned out,
the Aberdeen I.L.P. did not join the national party, but
before examining the reasons for this, it would be as well to
consider the organisation as it existed in Aberdeen in 1892-3,
when it was at its peak.

The social composition of the party was interesting. The
bulk of its members were trade unionists, and the strength
of the party amongst local trade union leaders was remarkable. This was brought out very clearly in a document
drawn up in February 1893 for presentation to Champion.
The document expressed continued confidence in Champion
and declared the signatories' 'concurrence with you in
distrust of both the great political parties, and in the belief
that the time has come when the consideration and practical
treatment of Labour questions, and notably the adoption of
an Eight Hours Bill must be forced on the attention of the
Imperial Parliament by means of an Independent Labour
Party . . .'. Sixty persons signed this statement: they
included prominent individual members of the Aberdeen
independent Labour organisation, and a number of miscellaneous trade unionists. Of the remaining signatories,
two—W. Diack and W. S. Rennie—were respectively

[1] *Daily Free Press*, 27 Mar. 1893.

secretary and treasurer of the Aberdeen Socialist Society, and no less than forty-one others were officials—chairmen, vice-presidents, secretaries, treasurers, or delegates to the Trades Councils—of local trade unions or union branches.[1] There were, for example, A. Catto and W. G. Smith, respectively chairman and secretary of the bakers' union branch; and J. Anderson and W. Maitland, respectively chairman and treasurer of the masons' union. Other unions whose officials figured prominently in the list were those of the granite polishers, blacksmiths, cabinetmakers, sawmillers, slaters, tinplate workers, boot and shoe operatives, bookbinders, combmakers, and farm servants—the latter, in Aberdeen, being general labourers. Other evidence corroborates the impression that these particular unions in Aberdeen were independent Labour in their political outlook. It seems to have been mainly the newly formed or re-formed unions, whether of skilled or unskilled workers, which adopted this leftist attitude, whilst several of the older unions, such as the ironmoulders', engineers', boilermakers', and joiners', remained Liberal or neutral in politics. Curiously enough, the list of independent Labour supporters included the names of the chairman and secretary of the amalgamated joiners', the chairman of the amalgamated tailors', and the secretary of the Scottish tailors' union branches, but the balance of evidence goes to show that these organisations were predominantly Liberal.

The strength of the independent Labour men in the Trades Council was overwhelming in 1893: of the sixty men who signed the document for presentation to Champion, at least twenty-five were members of the Council in that year —and the Council also included three or four Socialists who had not signed, together with many delegates who were not decidedly Liberal in their outlook. More impressive still, the sixty signatories included the president, vice-president, secretary, treasurer, and thirteen of the remaining

---

[1] *Aberdeen Labour Elector*, 11 Feb. 1893. In some cases, the union positions occupied by these men were held at the time of the General Election of 1892; in other cases, they were acquired between then and February 1893.

twenty-one members of the executive committee of the
Trades Council elected in January 1893—and of the eight
executive committee members unaccounted for, one was
J. Leatham, and another was J. Stephen, a slater who was a
member of the Aberdeen I.L.P. but who had not signed this
particular document.

Other sections of the community, besides trade unionists,
were attracted by the party. The *Aberdeen Labour Elector*
claimed that it was 'composed of students, lawyers, jour-
nalists, doctors, business men, mechanics, and labourers',[1]
and although the middle-class members were not very
numerous they occupied a disproportionately large place in
the leadership of the party. Partly, no doubt, this was due
to the fact that working-men were virtually barred from
membership of the Town Council by reason of that body's
meetings being held during the day-time, and therefore
middle-class men loomed large as electoral representatives
of the party. Probably the prominent position in the party
occupied by professional men was due mainly to the peculiar
evolution of the organisation: it had evolved, without a
break, from the Aberdeen Labour Committee which itself
was made up of a group of men who had largely led the
Junior Liberal Association. The Labour Committee had
been composed entirely of men who were ineligible for
membership of a trade union: they were G. Bisset, an erstwhile trade unionist, but now an employer; G. Gerrie, a
fairly well-to-do bank official who usually contrived to keep
out of the public eye, and gained a reputation as a wire-
puller; Dr. A. T. G. Beveridge and Dr. (later Sir) W. L.
Mackenzie, both medical men; W. C. Spence, a schoolteacher; A. P. Glass, a shopkeeper-hatter; W. C. Mitchell,
a clerk; A. Birse, a retired schoolteacher; and the Rev. A.
Webster, Unitarian minister. In 1893, the executive committee of the Aberdeen I.L.P. included all these men, with
the exception of Mackenzie and Webster, both of whom had
left Aberdeen, and Spence: Beveridge was chairman of the
party, Mitchell one of its joint-secretaries, and Gerrie its

---

[1] *Aberdeen Labour Elector*, 28 Jan. 1893.

organising spirit. In addition, the executive committee consisted of the vice-chairman of the party, J. Keir (who was also vice-president of the Trades Council); the treasurer, J. Philip, a trade unionist; the other joint-secretary, J. I. Mundie, a wood-sawyer and also a trade unionist; and J. Smith, who was apparently not a trade unionist. This list of the members of the executive committee is probably incomplete, however.[1]

Clearly, the Aberdeen I.L.P. had the makings of a large party, and, not unnaturally, it was inclined to over-estimate its strength. The *Aberdeen Labour Elector* went so far as to claim, in 1893, that the Aberdeen Town Council was 'the only body of the kind in the United Kingdom in which the Labour interest is the dominant force'. This interesting claim was based on an analysis of the membership of the Town Council, distinguishing between four groups of members: the first group consisted of five who were members of the I.L.P.—Bisset (who was now City Treasurer), Beveridge, Johnston, Glass, and Gray; the second group comprised nine men 'who may be relied on in most cases to vote with the Labour members'; then there were seven members of the Town Council 'who may be relied on to vote against the Labour members on all vital points (men who should be knocked out neck and crop at the earliest opportunity)'; and lastly, eleven 'Doubtfuls and Squeezables (chiefly, though not exclusively, men without ideas)'.[2] This was soon proved to be a highly optimistic estimate. The third group certainly came up to expectations, but that was all: the second group could not, in fact, be relied upon; the 'doubtfuls' were very doubtful indeed, and the 'squeezables' very slippery or else subject to other pressures; and even the five

---

[1] W. C. Mitchell, at different times in the 'nineties, was a member of an insurance agents' union, the General Labourers' Union, and the Farm Servants' Union. J. I. Mundie, before coming to Aberdeen in 1892, had been a district organiser of the London dockers' union in Dundee; in Aberdeen, he represented the wood-sawyers on the Trades Council. A. P. Glass, incidentally, advertised himself in the *Aberdeen Labour Elector* not only as a hatter, hosier, and glover, but also as the maker of the 'Champion' dress shirt!

[2] *Aberdeen Labour Elector*, 7 Jan. 1893.

POLITICS

155

reality—Gray (a cab proprietor) had retained his membership of the Liberal party, and soon left the I.L.P.

Nevertheless, when all allowance has been made for
exaggeration, there can be no doubt that the Aberdeen
I.L.P. was a force to be reckoned with in 1892 and 1893. It
distributed 20,000 copies of a manifesto of its aims,[1] and it
was probably members of the party who were largely
responsible for the increase in political discussion and
activity in the trade unions at the time: the masons' union,
for example, was holding members' meetings for general
political discussion.[2] Perhaps as a result of declining support
for Liberalism, the Gladstonian *Northern Daily News* became
an evening newspaper, the *Northern Evening News*, in 1892,
and this in turn closed down completely in the spring of the
following year. There was an incident in connection with
this which is not likely to have raised the standing of the
Liberal party locally. Some of the compositors employed on
the *Northern Evening News* held £1 shares in the concern and
when it was wound up they accepted an offer of 5s. per share
made by P. Esslemont, M.P. for East Aberdeenshire: in
fact, however, the shares sold to Esslemont were worth
12s. 6d. each a few days later.[3]

Another measure of the strength of the independent
Labour movement in Aberdeen was the publication of a
weekly newspaper, the *Aberdeen Labour Elector*. The first
number of this appeared on 7 January 1893, and for three
months it was published as a supplement to the London
Labour Elector, which had been revived under the editorship
of M. Barry. From 1 April, however, the *Aberdeen Labour
Elector* existed in its own right and, with a change of name to

[1] *Aberdeen Labour Elector*, 28 Jan. 1893.
[2] J. Leatham, *loc. cit.* vol. XXIX, no. 343, p. 14. In May 1893, the masons'
union decided to hold its regular meetings monthly instead of quarterly
(*Aberdeen Labour Elector*, 13 May 1893).
[3] Esslemont was chairman of the company, though he acted in his individual
capacity—and through an intermediary—in making this deal. Leatham was
one of the compositors concerned, and he lost no time in publicising the story
(J. Leatham, *loc. cit.* vol. XXIX, no. 343, pp. 15-16).

that of the *Aberdeen Standard* from 7 September, it continued
to appear regularly until February 1894.[1] The paper was
attractively written, and, although its references to prominent Liberals were often scathing, it sometimes showed
signs of a moderating influence; for example, its opinion of
the Aberdeen Conciliation Board was that it 'may not be
infallible, but it is commendably fair and just to both sides'.[2]
In reality, the paper was less the organ of the Aberdeen
I.L.P. than of H. H. Champion, who almost certainly
subsidised it.

Champion was the dominating influence in the Aberdeen
party, of which he was honorary president, and to him must
go much of the responsibility both for the growth of the
party and for its decline from the latter part of 1893.
Champion's position in the national Independent Labour
movement in that year steadily deteriorated. He had missed
the foundation conference of the I.L.P. at Bradford, and was
not a member of the National Administrative Council of the
new party elected there. But Champion had no intention of
being ignored, and early in 1893 he proved a constant source
of embarrassment to the leadership of the party, especially
as he had access to sources of money which were suspected
to be Tory. When Champion intervened, on his own
initiative but in the name of the I.L.P., in a by-election at
Grimsby, Keir Hardie and most of the members of the
National Administrative Council felt compelled to issue a
public repudiation of him. The struggle which then ensued
between Champion and most of the I.L.P. leaders—represented mainly by Keir Hardie—was primarily one of
democratic control: was the I.L.P. to be represented, in the
eyes of the public, by its elected leadership or by Champion?
To the leaders of the party it was vital that this issue should
be settled quickly, since Champion was constantly being

---

[1] Apart from two missing numbers, a complete file of the *Aberdeen Labour
Elector*, with a few copies of the *Aberdeen Standard*, is in King's College Library,
Aberdeen; the British Museum has a file of the *Aberdeen Standard* from 7 Sep.
1893 to 3 Feb. 1894, but not of its predecessor.

[2] *Aberdeen Labour Elector*, 4 Mar. 1893.

accused by Liberals of being a Tory, and it would be highly prejudicial to the future of the new party if such an accusation came to be levelled against it.

As far as Champion was concerned, there was a grain of truth in the accusation. Besides the question of certain aspects of his policy, he was very closely and openly associated with Maltman Barry, a self-confessed Conservative party man who was active in the Labour movement.[1] Moreover, Champion had a remarkable ability for securing money to finance candidatures: he found the money for the expenses of John Burns' candidature for Nottingham in 1885, and he offered Hardie money for the election funds of the Scottish Labour party candidates in 1892. This latter offer was refused, since it was subject to certain conditions: Champion was to be satisfied beforehand as to the suitability of the candidates, he was to sanction each item of expenditure, and there was to be no public concealment of the fact that Champion was providing the money.[2] In effect, Champion was trying to buy control of the Independent Labour movement. He was probably sincere in his ambition to build a new party independent of both the older ones, but the sources from which he derived his oft-profferred money were not above suspicion of ulterior motives: part of the money certainly came from a friend, R. W. Hudson, a soap magnate and Liberal Unionist opponent of Gladstone, and part may have come from unknown sources via Barry.

In his struggle against Hardie, Champion received the support of the Aberdeen I.L.P. Up to the time of the open breach between the two men, the Aberdeen party had intended to join the national I.L.P., and it was in no way hostile to Hardie—indeed, Hardie addressed one of its

---

[1] Barry was editor of the *Labour Elector* in 1893, and conceivably also of the *Aberdeen Labour Elector*. He stood as a Conservative Democrat for Banffshire in the General Election of 1892, but was defeated.

[2] J. Burgess, *John Burns: The Rise and Progress of a Right Honourable* (1911), pp. 17, 151; *Aberdeen Labour Elector*, 29 April 1893; 6 May 1893. Champion also arranged for donations of £100 to the election funds of each of four Labour candidates (including Hardie) in London in 1892.

meetings on 3 April 1893, and was well received.[1] From then onwards, however, the *Aberdeen Labour Elector* attacked Hardie in increasingly sharp terms,[2] and on 8 May Champion, at a meeting of the Aberdeen I.L.P., successfully vindicated himself, apparently meeting no opposition.[3] Champion also received support from a few prominent Labour leaders in Scotland, such as J. L. Mahon, who had been associated with him for several years, and R. Chisholm Robertson, the miners' leader and former secretary of the Scottish Trades Councils' Labour party, who had a personal feud with Hardie. With the co-operation of these men, Champion made a desperate attempt to regain his waning influence by reviving the Scottish Trades Councils' Labour party. When this party had been dissolved in March, a small committee had been appointed to arrange for an annual conference of all independent Labour organisations. The committee consisted of Champion's supporters, and he used it to promote a Scottish Labour conference in Dundee on 7 October 1893.

The conference was a failure: Keir Hardie had not been invited to attend, and most Scottish Labour party branches boycotted the meeting. Only five Trades Councils, including that of Aberdeen, were represented. Of the twenty-three delegates present, five were from the Aberdeen I.L.P., and six from the Dundee Scottish Labour party: it was soon apparent that these, the two largest delegations, were at cross purposes. The ostensible object of the conference was to consider means of consolidating the Labour vote in Scotland before the next General Election, and Champion's supporters wanted an executive committee to be appointed

---

[1] *Daily Free Press*, 4 April 1893. Hardie was careful to avoid reference to Champion at this meeting.

[2] E.g. 'Mr. Hardie demands that Mr. Champion shall hand over his purse and his soul to the Council of the I.L.P. . . . "Your money or your life" is, in short, the modest demand made by Messrs. Hardie and Burgess' (*Aberdeen Labour Elector*, 29 April 1893).

[3] *Aberdeen Labour Elector*, 13 May 1893. Champion argued that the dispute was over policy: he wanted the party to be entirely independent, whereas Hardie, who had obtained his parliamentary seat with Liberal support, 'could not afford to act quite independently'.

for this purpose. This foreshadowed precisely what Hardie had predicted as the real object of the conference: an attempt to form a new Labour party, under Champion's guidance, to supersede the Scottish Labour party and the I.L.P. The delegates from Dundee were suspicious of Champion's motives, and the latter was able to gain some measure of unity only by dropping the suggestion of an executive committee. Instead, a committee was appointed with the task of requesting the Scottish Labour party to convene another conference of Labour organisations: if the Scottish Labour party did not do so, the committee, with Champion at its head, was itself to convene such a conference.[1] The committee was still-born. Champion had played his last card and lost: he left Britain for Australia in January 1894, and never returned.

Champion left behind him, in the Aberdeen I.L.P., a legacy of hostility to Keir Hardie and of isolation from the national Independent Labour movement. For the greater part of the four or five years of life left to it, the party in Aberdeen remained unattached to the national I.L.P. It seems likely that this isolation and the hostility to Hardie stemmed mainly from the middle-class leaders in Aberdeen. The Trades Council, for all its independent Labour majority, showed no sign of enmity towards Hardie: in 1893, it took no active part in the struggle between him and Champion; it sent a delegate to the Dundee conference, but the delegate chosen was W. Cooper, a member of the Aberdeen Socialist Society, and the Council defeated an attempt to instruct Cooper to propose a motion along the lines desired by Champion;[2] and the Council declined an invitation to send a delegate to the annual conference of the Scottish Labour party, but this was 'in consequence of the want of funds and not as a result of any lack of sympathy'.[3] In 1894, when Hardie, in order to draw attention to a mining disaster, opposed a parliamentary vote of congratulation to the

---

[1] *Daily Free Press*, 9 Oct. 1893; *Aberdeen Labour Elector*, 12 Oct. 1893.
[2] *Minutes*, 27 Sep. 1893. Cooper was left with a free hand.
[3] *Ibid.* 22 Nov. 1893.

Queen upon the birth of a child to the Duchess of York, the Aberdeen Trades Council congratulated him upon his 'bold and courageous stand'.[1]

From the latter part of 1893, the Aberdeen I.L.P. showed increasing signs of weakness and loss of influence. In part, this may be attributed to the removal of the dominant personality of Champion and to isolation from the national movement. Other factors doubtless had their effect. The party had been built up rapidly on the basis of a programme of immediate reforms, such as the statutory eight-hour day, which were not achieved: unlike the local branch of the S.D.F., it had no fundamental social philosophy to fall back on to refresh its faith when little or no progress was being made. Its methods were rather those of the old-established political parties than those of a new and vigorous one, and were not well calculated to sustain, in difficult circumstances, the initial enthusiasm of members of the party: again, unlike the S.D.F., it did not indulge in ceaseless propagandist activity but relied upon occasional public meetings with an extra burst of activities during elections. There had been comment upon this in the *Aberdeen Labour Elector* as early as April 1893. 'The Party has been resting on its oars rather long, and should now wake up a bit. It should endeavour to get amongst the people more. It is all very well to be calm and avoid the vulgarisms of mere demagogism, but political sobriety can be practised without acquiring political "respectability".'[2]

Internal dissension added its quota of difficulty. Bisset resigned from the party in September 1893, ostensibly because he preferred local veto rather than municipalisation as a solution to the drink problem. Beveridge, however, alleged that Bisset had constantly differed from the other Labour town councillors and had 'acted as a drag and a

---

[1] *Minutes*, 4 July 1894. On the other hand, Beveridge, chairman of the Aberdeen I.L.P., criticised Hardie's action in this connection (*Daily Free Press*, 5 Sep. 1894).

[2] *Aberdeen Labour Elector*, 1 April 1893. A Labour Church was established in Aberdeen late in 1893, but was short-lived.

wet blanket' on them.[1] In the municipal elections of that year, the Aberdeen I.L.P. and the Trades Council jointly sponsored four candidates, only one of whom, W. Johnston, was elected. Bisset had aided this 'rout of the Labourist party'[2] by publicly supporting opposing candidates, and the Trades Council recognised the breach between Bisset and his erstwhile trade union brothers by expressing regret at his attitude.[3] At about the same time, the Trades Council condemned G. Gerrie for attempted interference in its affairs.[4]

When the time came for the municipal elections of 1894, the Aberdeen I.L.P. had declined so far as to be unable, on the grounds of expense, to put forward any candidates.[5] The party was not unimportant, and the Tory sympathies of some of its members call for special consideration, but henceforth it was but a shadow of its former self. It died away quietly in 1897 or 1898, and was not resuscitated until ten years later. However, the steady decline of the party organisation did not mean any change in the political complexion of the Aberdeen Trades Council. There the independent Labour supporters remained strongly in the majority, and the years from 1893 to 1895 witnessed a constant struggle between this dominant group and the Liberal minority.[6] Two incidents in this struggle may

[1] *Daily Free Press*, 1 Nov. 1893; 5 Sep. 1893; 3 Oct. 1893.

[2] Editorial comment in *Daily Free Press*, 8 Nov. 1893. As before, this was largely wishful thinking: in April 1894, four out of five Trades Council candidates were successful in the School Board elections.

[3] *Minutes*, 8 Nov. 1893; 23 Nov. 1893. The motion expressing 'regret' was carried very narrowly—twenty-five votes to twenty-four—against a proposal to condemn Bisset for his 'treachery to the cause of the workers'.

[4] *Ibid.* 7 Oct. 1893; 11 Oct. 1893.

[5] *Daily Free Press*, 3 Oct. 1894. Keir and others brought this despondent attitude into the Trades Council by proposing that, on the score of expense, no candidates should be nominated by it. Most members of the Council disagreed: two candidates were nominated, one of whom, J. I. Mundie, was elected (*Minutes*, 26 Sep. 1894; 2 Oct. 1894).

[6] Lest it be thought that the dominant position of the advocates of independent Labour in 1893 was due simply to the withdrawal from the Council of the delegates of some Liberal-minded trade unions, it should be mentioned that a strikingly large number of delegates in that year were new to the Council. Most of these newcomers were independent Labour in outlook, and their presence perhaps reflects changes of political opinion in many unions.

be singled out as evidence of the remarkable change which had come over the Council in the space of a few years.

In 1886, the Trades Council had expressed approval of Gladstone's first Irish Home Rule Bill. Seven years later, it discussed Gladstone's second attempt to carry the measure. The Parliamentary Bills Committee of the Council recommended that no action be taken in connection with the Bill, and this recommendation of neutrality was accepted—on a vote of twenty-two to twenty—by the Council.[1] Livingston, however, was dissatisfied with this, and at the next meeting he proposed that the Council petition in favour of the Home Rule Bill, claiming that 'it was a measure not only necessary for Ireland but also for Scotland'. The ensuing discussion revealed a division of opinion amongst the independent Labour members of the Council. Catto and Keir moved an amendment 'that the Council simply approve of the principle of Home Rule': Catto expressed criticism of the details of the Bill. Mundie, however, went further than this by moving an amendment re-affirming the Council's neutrality in the matter, and he said that the Council 'would do quite unnecessary work' if it carried Catto's amendment. W. C. Mitchell supported Mundie, arguing that 'if the Bill was passed in its present form a fancy franchise would be established and also a Second Chamber both of which no democrat could support'. The two amendments were put against each other: Mundie's received twenty-nine votes and Catto's twenty-five. Mundie's amendment was then carried against Livingston's motion by thirty-six votes to nineteen. In effect, most members of the Council were expressing their conviction that social legislation was more important than 'political' measures.[2]

---

[1] *Minutes*, 26 April 1893; *Daily Free Press*, 27 April 1893. Livingston arrived at the meeting only at the tail-end of this part of the business.

[2] *Minutes*, 10 May 1893. Champion's influence may be seen in this. There was an undercurrent of implied anti-Irish feeling in the *Labour Elector* and the *Aberdeen Labour Elector* in 1893: a feeling of resentment that the Irish issue—which, in Champion's view, was not of great importance to British workers—should be allowed to dominate the field of politics.

Less than a year after this, a situation rather similar in character developed. In 1886, Livingston had moved the Trades Council to declare itself unanimously in favour of the abolition of the House of Lords.[1] In 1893-4, there was again conflict between the two Houses of Parliament. The Liberal government was redeeming its promise to bring in an Employers' Liability Bill; the measure passed through the Commons, but the Lords interpolated a clause enabling employers to contract out of its provisions. The Bill was then bandied back and forth between the two Houses until 13 February 1894, when the Liberal majority in the Commons agreed to make a concession to the other House: in effect, contracting out of the Bill was to be allowed for a period of three years after its passage into law. Gladstone secured a very narrow majority in the Commons for this concession, several Liberal M.P.s opposing it, whilst a number of Irish Nationalist M.P.s were absent. At this point Livingston, in the Aberdeen Trades Council, moved the suspension of standing orders—since he had not given notice of motion— to enable him to propose that 'in view of the long continued obstruction by the House of Lords . . . we believe the time has now come when this continual friction between the accredited representatives of the people and the representatives of privilege and monopoly should cease and we therefore urge on the government to take the necessary steps to end this monstrous anomaly'. But this was 1894, not 1886: the Council refused to suspend standing orders, and Livingston therefore had to give notice of his motion for a future meeting. The Council did suspend standing orders, however, to enable W. C. Mitchell to put a motion condemning 'those professed friends of labour' who had been absent from the debate in the Commons on 13 February, and also those M.P.s who had voted in favour of the compromise then proposed by the government on the

[1] *Minutes*, 7 July 1886. See also a resolution of 1884: 'that the power vested in the House [of Lords] of vetoing measures passed by the House of Commons ought to be abolished' (*Minutes*, 13 Aug. 1884).

Employers' Liability Bill. This motion was agreed upon unanimously.[1]

Before the next meeting of the Trades Council, the House of Lords had rejected the compromise offered by Gladstone, who then abandoned the Bill. The Council considered a recommendation from its executive committee that it should condemn the action of the Liberal party in dropping the Bill and should urge 'the necessity of pressing forward measures which have the approval of organised labour of the nation until such measures are carried, or the House of Lords abolished'. The Council adopted the first part of this recommendation but deleted the reference to the House of Lords.[2] Times had indeed changed, when the Council, instead of adopting the simple course of condemning the House of Lords, could thus turn the attack against the Liberal party for compromising with the upper House and its Tory majority.

The final stage in the development of this incident was reached on 28 March when Livingston, who was nothing if not persistent, proposed the motion of which he had given notice six weeks earlier, calling for an end to the 'monstrous anomaly'—the House of Lords. In opposition, Mitchell moved an amendment 'that the Council decline to identify itself with the agitation until a definite scheme had been laid before them by a responsible government as to what institution if any should take the place of the present House of Lords'. This amendment attracted forty-three votes, against only eight for Livingston's motion.[3] The significance of this majority became clearer later in the year, when the Trades Council's delegate to the annual T.U.C. conference

[1] *Minutes*, 14 Feb. 1894. According to the *Daily Free Press*, 14 Feb. 1894, the second part of Mitchell's motion condemned those M.P.s who had voted *against* the compromise proposed by the Liberal government.

[2] *Minutes*, 28 Feb. 1894. The executive committee itself had decided upon the reference to the House of Lords only on the casting vote of the president (*Minutes*, 21 Feb. 1894).

[3] *Ibid.* 28 Mar. 1894. Gladstone was not spoiling for a constitutional struggle with the upper House, but the Council of the Aberdeen Liberal Association, meeting on 28 Feb. 1894, demanded the speedy abolition of the House of Lords.

ALEXANDER CATTO (*c.* 1910)

was instructed, 'in connection with the resolution calling for the abolition of the House of Lords, to move the entire abolition of a Second Chamber';[1] the Trades Council was aware of the danger that the House of Lords might be replaced by another undemocratic, if more innocuous, institution of government.

The dog fight between Liberal and independent Labour members of the Trades Council continued into 1895, when it became necessary for the Council to declare its attitude in the General Election of that year. It was at this time that tendencies towards Conservatism on the part of a number of leaders of the Aberdeen I.L.P. came clearly into the open, and it is worth examining the development of these tendencies. There had been some signs of such a development in the Trades Council in the 'eighties, over the question of free trade or protection. There was little chance of an openly protectionist policy receiving much support in the Council, but 'fair trade' proposals achieved a measure of success. In 1880, the Council received a deputation, led by J. McLean of Greenock, from the Scottish Workmen's Society for the Abolition of Foreign Sugar Bounties.[2] The deputation asserted that foreign sugar bounties were injurious to British industry and should be met by a countervailing duty. 'They contended that there was nothing in this remedy antagonistic to the principles of Free Trade, in proof of which several eminent Free Trade Politicians were quoted.' The Council was satisfied, and a resolution was adopted condemning foreign sugar bounties and pledging the Council's co-operation in organising a public meeting in Aberdeen on the subject.[3]

A year later, the Council was invited by J. McLean to send a delegate to a conference organised by the National

---

[1] *Minutes*, 22 Aug. 1894; 29 Aug. 1894. The delegate was also instructed to support a motion urging the government to introduce the Employers' Liability Bill again at the earliest possible moment.

[2] This was actually a subsidiary of the National Anti-Bounty League, the organisation of the West India planting and British sugar-refining interests. Members of the League were associated with the National Fair Trade League. See B. H. Brown, *op. cit.* ch. 2.

[3] *Minutes*, 17 Nov. 1880. The public meeting was held on 31 Jan. 1881.

12

League to consider 'the depressed state of trade and industry of the United Kingdom'; the conference was to be held in London immediately before the T.U.C. conference there. The Council, which had already decided to send its secretary, Annand, to the latter conference, hesitated before accepting McLean's invitation: it was dubious about the resolutions which were to be submitted to the National League conference, and a lengthy discussion took place 'as to whether the resolutions were likely to compromise the Council in a departure from the principle of Free Trade'. However, eventually Annand was instructed to attend the conference.[1] Very little is known of his attitude at it. He may have been caught up in the attempt made later by the 'fair trade' elements to pack the T.U.C. conference, but if so he was almost certainly not one of those who were bribed to make the attempt, and he was not expelled from the T.U.C. When he returned to Aberdeen, he proposed acceptance of the view of the National League that the commercial treaty with France should not be renewed 'except on more favourable terms than the one [treaty] presently existing'. By a narrow majority, this proposal was rejected by the Trades Council.[2]

In 1888, the question of foreign sugar bounties was again discussed in the Council. An international sugar conference was taking place in London, and the London Trades Council was agitating against the bounty system. The Aberdeen Trades Council sent delegates to meetings on the subject, convened by the London Trades Council both in Dundee and in London;[3] and in July, when the Aberdeen Council heard that a draft convention had been initialled at the international conference, binding signatory powers to abolish export bounties on sugar, it expressed its gratification and trusted that the government would 'maintain the clause in such convention which excludes from the markets of other

---

[1] *Minutes*, 5 Sep. 1881. The National League was an offshoot of the National Fair Trade League, and was designed to attract working-class support.
[2] *Ibid.* 14 Sep. 1881. Annand was, and remained, a Liberal.
[3] *Ibid.* 18 Jan. 1888; 22 Feb. 1888.

countries the bounty-aided products of any nation which does not conform to the provisions of the treaty'.[1] Here, indeed, was the thin end of the wedge of protection, in the form of a threat of countervailing duties; yet it was W. Livingston who moved this resolution. The sugar-bounty issue provides a good illustration of the way in which many Liberal workers found themselves supporting a movement which, while nominally advocating an extension of free trade—to other countries—had protectionist implications. However, such implications in the anti-bounty movement were not fully apparent, and it was not inseparably associated with the general 'fair trade' agitation: the sugar lobby would have been quite content to have its own narrow interests settled apart from those of the other protectionist groups.[2]

A little earlier than this, a more openly protectionist move had been made by some members of the Aberdeen Trades Council. Coutts, a compositor, and W. Leys (a Conservative) asked the Council to endorse their view that 'the present fiscal policy of this country is prejudicial to the interests of the working classes, and demands the attention of government, with a view to a rearrangement which will place it in a position of equality in competing with other nations'. Bisset and Thompson were not content merely to oppose this motion: they proposed to add to it the words, 'by the abolition of all custom and excise duties'. Bisset's view was that there was too little free trade, and that all duties, including non-protectionist ones, should be abolished; and his proposal was adopted, in spite of Leys' protest that it simply meant free trade in drink.[3]

In advocating a 'fair trade' policy, Leys reflected the general trend of opinion amongst Conservatives. The

[1] *Minutes*, 11 July 1888. As it happened, the draft convention was not ratified, owing to Liberal opposition.

[2] E.g. R. A. MacFie, a Scottish sugar-refining industrialist, left the National Fair Trade League in the mid-'eighties because he felt unable to support a duty on foodstuffs (B. H. Brown, *op. cit.* p. 23).

[3] *Minutes*, 2 Feb. 1887; *Daily Free Press*, 3 Feb. 1887. P. Milne, an orthodox Liberal, moved the previous question, but failed to find a seconder.

Scottish Union of Conservative Associations voted in favour of protection in July 1887,[1] and this feeling was naturally prominent in the north-east of Scotland,[2] where Conservatism had a marked rural bias. The extent to which industry in Aberdeen was affected by foreign competition in the 'eighties is not at all clear. The only indication available is contained in the submission by the Aberdeen Chamber of Commerce to the Royal Commission on Depression of Trade and Industry. According to the Chamber, 'the produce of most of the manufacturing trades and industries [of Aberdeen and surrounding district] is disposed of in about equal proportions in the home and foreign markets, the spinning and manufacturing of flax to all parts of the world, the spinning of cotton entirely to India'. Local trade and industry were affected 'seriously' by foreign competition, and 'to a large extent' by foreign tariffs and bounties:[3] but the Chamber of Commerce did not go beyond these generalisations, and there may not be much reality in them. There was greater reason for alarm later, in the 'nineties, when the effects of the McKinley tariff in particular were felt in some industries.

The signs, in the 'eighties, of a movement of opinion towards protectionism amongst members of the Aberdeen Trades Council did not amount to very much and did not indicate a real growth of Conservative influence. A new element was introduced, however, when H. H. Champion established his connection with Aberdeen. Champion's social background was more Tory than Liberal, and he had no dogmatic objection to protection as a policy. He did not openly advocate protection, but as early as 1888 he stated that workers could not hope for an eight-hour day 'without conceding the *principle* of Fair Trade'.[4] In the General Election campaign of 1892, when Champion was being

---

[1] B. H. Brown, *op. cit.* p. 67.

[2] See A. Forbes, *Free Imports and Agricultural Ruin, or Protection and Prosperity* (Pamphlet, published in Aberdeen, 1888; in Public Library, Aberdeen).

[3] *Royal Commission on Depression of Trade and Industry*, 1886, First Report [C. 4621], p. 74.

[4] Quoted by B. H. Brown, *op. cit.* p. 30, from *Fair Trade*, 2 Mar. 1888.

accused by his opponents of being a Tory and a protectionist, he could do no more than repeat arguments first elaborated some years before: protection, he said, was desirable, in connection with the eight-hour day, only in those British industries whose technical equipment and organisation were equal to those of similar industries abroad but which nevertheless were subject to unfair competition from relatively cheap foreign labour.[1] The emphasis of the argument was on cheap foreign labour, and Champion's views soon found currency in the independent Labour movement in Aberdeen.

To some extent, the ground had already been prepared for these views. In 1887, the Aberdeen Trades Council, in response to a letter from the Glasgow Trades Council, expressed strong disapproval of the action of an Ayrshire steel-works in bringing into the country a number of Poles 'and by means of them forcing down the wages of their labourers to starvation point'. The resolution, moved by Bisset, went on to urge the Parliamentary Committee of the T.U.C. to bring before Parliament the whole question of immigration into Britain, 'with a view to having it stopped so long as a million of our fellow countrymen are without the means of earning a livelihood'. In his speech, Bisset also contrasted immigration with continuing emigration from Britain.[2]

In February 1893, a shoemakers' delegate to the Trades Council proposed 'That in the opinion of the Council the excessive influx of pauper alien labour, which by unfair competition displaces native labour, has a tendency to reduce wages and makes the condition of labour generally unbearable, calls for immediate legislative interference'. Catto seconded this, and although W. Cooper opposed, arguing that the only remedy for the evil was the socialisation of the means of production, the motion was carried by a large majority.[3] One month later, the annual conference

---

[1] The *Fiery Cross*, 30 June 1892 (in Public Library, Aberdeen); *Nineteenth Century*, Sep. 1889.
[2] *Minutes*, 21 Dec. 1887.   [3] *Ibid.* 15 Feb. 1893.

12 *

of the Scottish Trades Councils' Labour party adopted a resolution framed in similar terms;[1] and in 1894 the Trades Council decided to petition in favour of a Bill, introduced by Unionist M.P.s, designed to stop imports of goods made in foreign prisons.[2]

The stage was thus set for a full-scale debate in the Trades Council on the issue of protection. On 25 September 1895, Catto, seconded by Forbes, moved 'That in view of the great injury done to a large number of trades by the whole-sale importation of foreign manufactured goods made under unfair conditions the Council petition Her Majesty's Government to reconsider their fiscal policy with the view of protecting our home industries'. In urging this motion, Catto emphasised its connection with the demand for an eight-hour day, and reminded delegates that they had objected to the influx of pauper aliens: why should they not object to goods made by pauper aliens in their own countries? Livingston rose to the challenge, and moved an amendment re-affirming support for the principle of free trade. When a vote was taken, the Council divided evenly, motion and amendment each receiving twenty votes. Keir—who, like Catto and Forbes, was a prominent member of the Aberdeen I.L.P.—gave his casting vote in favour of Catto's motion. At that point, however, A. Robertson, who was a member of the S.D.F., moved another amendment: 'That this Council petition Her Majesty's Government to limit by legislation the royalties and rents in Great Britain in order to secure to our manufacturers the raw material at a price that will admit of our competing in the markets of the world with the manufacturers of other countries.' When this amendment was voted on, it received thirty votes as against seventeen for the original motion, and it was therefore declared to be the view of the Council.[3]

[1] *Aberdeen Labour Elector*, 1 April 1893. The Aberdeen Trades Council brought the question up again in 1898, at the Scottish T.U.C., but received no support from other delegates (*Minutes*, 9 Mar. 1898; 5 May 1898).

[2] *Minutes*, 20 June 1894. The President of the Board of Trade replied that the quantity of such goods imported was insignificant (*Minutes*, 4 July 1894).

[3] *Ibid.* 25 Sep. 1895; *Daily Free Press*, 26 Sep. 1895.

Clearly, then, on this important question of fiscal policy a number of independent Labour supporters held opinions which approximated to those prevalent in the Conservative party. It was noticeable also, in the early 'nineties, that many leaders of the Aberdeen I.L.P. were more concerned to criticise the Liberal than the Conservative party; and the *Aberdeen Labour Elector* gave sympathetic reports of interviews with Lord Provost Stewart and Sir Archibald Grant, both of whom were prominent local Conservatives.[1] To a considerable extent, the relatively greater vehemence of independent Labour attacks upon the Liberal party was natural in the circumstances: the leaders of the new party were ex-Liberals, embittered by failure to achieve their ends in the older party, and Liberalism, strongly entrenched in Aberdeen, must have seemed to them a greater immediate enemy than Conservatism. Yet there was more to it than that. There was at least one tangible link between the Aberdeen I.L.P. and the Conservative party, in the person of Maltman Barry. Barry was no stranger to the Labour movement in Aberdeen; he had addressed the Trades Council on the subject of the eight-hour day in 1890,[2] and he may have been the editor of the *Aberdeen Labour Elector*. Besides being intimately associated with Champion, he was acknowledged by G. Gerrie as 'a very close personal friend'.[3] The importance of this link was demonstrated in 1894-5.

On 12 May 1894, there was a conference between representatives of the Aberdeen Trades Council, I.L.P., and S.D.F., to consider the Parliamentary representation of the two constituencies in the city. The conference made three recommendations, and these were later considered by the Trades Council. The first recommendation was to express dissatisfaction with the two Liberal M.P.s; this was adopted by the Council on a vote of thirty-six to eighteen—about half

[1] *Aberdeen Labour Elector*, 18 May 1893; 13 July 1893. E.g. Stewart 'has a singularly broad conception of the good of the community as a whole, rather than of the selfish interests of any class in it. . . .'
[2] *Minutes*, 6 Aug. 1890; 20 Aug. 1890.   [3] *Daily Free Press*, 15 June 1891.

of the eighteen opponents being Liberals, the remainder
favouring a neutral attitude. The second recommendation
was that 'a strong effort should be made to find Labour
candidates for both divisions of the city'. This also was
adopted, but only by the narrow margin of twenty-seven
votes to twenty-three: Mundie, an independent Labour
supporter, having seen the strength of the opposition to the
first recommendation, opposed the second 'in the interests
of the Trades Council and Trade Unionism . . . he believed
this work could be done more effectively outside the Council'.
The third recommendation was that, in the event of no
Labour candidates being found, Conservative candidates
should be supported, 'if they were prepared to go as far on
labour questions as the Liberal candidates'.[1]

This novel proposition had come from the Aberdeen
I.L.P. representatives at the original joint conference, and
had been opposed then by the representatives of the local
S.D.F. These divergent views were reflected in the Trades
Council, until at length Diack (a Socialist) successfully
moved to defer a decision on the recommendation, on the
ground that it was premature.[2] As to the reasons for the
attitude of the I.L.P., Mundie had supported the proposal
on tactical grounds: the Tories were weaker than the
Liberals, and should therefore be supported temporarily if
there were no Labour candidates.[3] Beveridge, chairman of
the I.L.P., went rather further: 'Comparing the rival
programmes of the parties, one could not fail to see that the
working classes had at present much more to hope for from
the Conservative than the Liberal party. . . . There could
not be a doubt that the Conservatives would be returned,
and why should not the Labour party share the spoils? . . .'[4]

The tactical design of the manœuvre became clearer in
July 1894, when Maltman Barry addressed a public meeting
of the Aberdeen Conservative Association. Barry was being
considered as a possible Conservative candidate for the

[1] *Minutes*, 6 June 1894.   [2] *Ibid.* 20 June 1894.
[3] *Daily Free Press*, 14 May 1894.
[4] Speech by Beveridge, quoted in *Daily Free Press*, 26 Mar. 1895.

constituency of South Aberdeen, and the meeting was held
to enable him to expound his views to local Conservatives—
although it was noted that some Labour leaders were also
in the audience. In his speech, Barry put forward several
familiar points of orthodox Conservative policy, such as the
need to maintain and bind together the Empire, but he also
advocated old age pensions and a statutory eight-hour day.[1]
Later events made it clear that the leaders of the Aberdeen
I.L.P. were hoping that Barry would be adopted as Conservative candidate for South Aberdeen; they themselves
intended to promote J. L. Mahon as independent Labour
candidate for North Aberdeen, and it was assumed that
both Barry and Mahon would have straight fights against
the Liberal candidates.

The plan came unstuck. Barry was not adopted by the
Aberdeen Conservative Association, which preferred a more
orthodox candidate in the person of Lord Provost Stewart.
In June 1895, moreover, there was talk of a Conservative
candidate being brought forward to contest North Aberdeen.
Stung by this disregard for its interests, the executive committee of the Aberdeen I.L.P. decided to recommend the
party to withdraw Mahon's candidature—since it was
considered that he had no chance in a three-cornered
struggle—and to support the return of the Liberal candidates.[2] But by the time this recommendation came to be
considered by a meeting of the I.L.P., the circumstances
had again changed: it was now known that there would
be no Conservative candidate for North Aberdeen. Consequently, the meeting was thrown into confusion; eventually,
it decided to nominate Mahon for North Aberdeen and to
support D. Stewart, the Conservative, in the south division,
though there was considerable opposition to this latter
decision.[3]

The Trades Council was equally riven by contending
groups. It had decided to make a test question of the legal

[1] *Daily Free Press*, 19 July 1894.   [2] *Ibid.* 29 June 1895.
[3] *Ibid.* 9 July 1895; 10 July 1895. Stewart was a Liberal Unionist, but he
was put up by the Conservative party organisation.

eight-hour day,[1] and a deputation was appointed to ascertain
the views of the candidates for South Aberdeen, Bryce and
Stewart, on the subject.[2] Of the two, Bryce (the Liberal)
was the more favourable: he maintained his standpoint that
a simple formula of eight hours for every man in all trades
was impracticable, but pointed out that he had voted for
the Miners' Eight-Hour Bill in Parliament. Stewart, on the
other hand, said that he would not oppose an experimental
eight-hour day for miners but favoured a general ten-hour,
rather than eight-hour, day.[3] When the deputation reported
back to the Trades Council—almost on the eve of the election—the independent Labour men were hopelessly split:
W. C. Mitchell and Forbes joined with Liberals to urge
support for Bryce, on the ground that he was more favourable towards the eight-hour day demand; Anderson and
Innes supported Stewart, presumably because the I.L.P.
had officially backed him; and Proctor joined with members
of the S.D.F. in enjoining neutrality on the part of the
Council in the South Aberdeen election. It was this last
proposal that was finally adopted, and the Council then
decided to take up a neutral attitude in North Aberdeen
as well.[4]

No doubt endorsement by the Trades Council of Mahon's
candidature could have been pushed through, and a few
independent Labour supporters made the attempt; but most
of the left-wing members of the Council thought it impolitic.
Keir, the president, himself moved the proposal that the
Council adopt a neutral attitude in North Aberdeen, and
agreed that 'it might seem inconsistent on his part to agree
to a recommendation to support Mr. Mahon in one body
[i.e. the I.L.P.] and not support Mr. Mahon in another
body. But many good trade unionists were much in favour

---

[1] *Minutes*, 1 May 1895; 5 June 1895; 3 July 1895.

[2] *Ibid.* 5 July 1895. Hunter and Mahon, the candidates for North
Aberdeen, were not interviewed: Mahon came into the field too late to make
it possible.

[3] *Daily Free Press*, 9 July 1895; 11 July 1895. The result of the deputation
to Stewart was known before the I.L.P. decided to support him.

[4] *Minutes*, 10 July 1895; 12 July 1895.

of Mr. Hunter, and in view of the diversity of opinion. . . .'¹ In spite of his late start, Mahon fought a vigorous campaign, but was badly defeated; he polled only 608 votes against Hunter's 4,156. Clearly, the bulk of the working-class still supported Hunter; and Mahon can have received few, if any, votes from Conservatives—although in the other constituency, where Bryce was returned with a reduced majority, Glass, Mundie, and Anderson (and Bisset) had addressed meetings in support of Stewart.²

The fiasco of this General Election sounded the death-knell of the Aberdeen I.L.P. It was discredited by its opportunism, and degenerated into a clique of prominent individuals rather than an organised political party. It remained influential, however, and the embers of the old feud with Keir Hardie still glowed in 1896. It was rumoured then that Hunter intended to resign his parliamentary seat for North Aberdeen and retire from politics. Hardie, who had lost his own seat the year before, was anxious to be adopted as Labour candidate for North Aberdeen if the rumour should prove true, and the national administrative council of the I.L.P. wrote to the Aberdeen Trades Council about the possible vacancy. In response, the Trades Council resolved that 'in the event of a by-election taking place the Council should show its willingness to give financial assistance and its undivided support to secure the return of a Labour Representative satisfactory to the Council, the local Independent Labour party and the Social Democratic Federation'. Forbes, an independent Labour supporter, moved this resolution; he said that there was talk of both Keir Hardie and Tom Mann as prospective candidates, and that 'to his mind either of these gentlemen would make excellent candidates'.³

In April 1896 there was a conference between representatives of the Trades Council, Aberdeen I.L.P., and

---

¹ *Daily Free Press*, 13 July 1895.
² The I.L.P. had issued a manifesto against Bryce, declaring that his opponent, Stewart, 'may not be an ideal candidate, but . . .' (*Daily Free Press*, 13 July 1895). ³ *Minutes*, 29 Jan. 1896.

S.D.F., at which it was agreed to recommend the adoption of Tom Mann as prospective candidate. There can be little doubt that the initiative in thus passing over the claims of Hardie came from the local I.L.P. Hardie himself had no doubts about it: 'There is, of course, a dead set against myself by the Gerrie clique.' [1] The Trades Council probably had no decided preference as between Mann and Hardie, but it did not want a repetition of the disunity amongst the local Labour forces which had been so apparent in the previous year. On 22 April 1896, Keir proposed that the Trades Council should adopt Mann as its candidate, praising him as 'a candidate who would unite all sections of the Labour movement', and hoping 'that they might show the Liberals and Conservatives that the workers for once were united and determined to return their candidate'. The Liberal element in the Council was completely routed on this occasion: Livingston tried to move a direct negative but failed to find a seconder, and Keir's motion was carried —it received forty-four votes against two for a delaying amendment. [2]

The new-found unity achieved enthusiastic expression in the whirlwind campaign conducted by Mann—there were only nine days between the publication of Hunter's decision to retire and polling day. In a straight fight, Mann was defeated by the Liberal candidate, D. V. Pirie, but the margin was narrow: Pirie polled 2,909 votes, and Mann 2,476. Keir had reason to declare to the Trades Council that 'the battle they had been engaged in had done more to raise the cause of labour than anything that had taken place in Aberdeen'. [3] Probably as a result of this electoral

---

[1] Letter from Hardie to Lowe, 20 Mar. 1896, quoted in D. Lowe, *From Pit to Parliament: The Story of the Early Life of James Keir Hardie* (1923), p. 98. Hardie was so disappointed that he seriously considered resigning the chairmanship of the I.L.P. (*ibid.* pp. 103-5).

[2] *Minutes*, 22 April 1896. Hunter's decision to apply for the Chiltern Hundreds had been made public by this time.

[3] *Ibid.* 6 May 1896. Mann's election programme included a maximum eight-hour day; raising of the age at which children were permitted to work; old age pensions; nationalisation of the land, of railways and waterways, mines and minerals, and municipalisation of docks; and a graduated income

struggle, the Aberdeen I.L.P. decided to join the national I.L.P., but the decision made no material contribution towards arresting the decline of the local party. Beveridge and Glass continued to hold their seats on the Aberdeen Town Council until after 1900, but they did so rather as prominent individual Labour men than as representatives of a party; W. Johnston also held his seat, though much more directly as a representative of the Trades Council, of which he was secretary.

From a political point of view, the three years which followed Mann's bid for the North Aberdeen seat were rather an anti-climax to the tumultuous years of the early 'nineties. Most of the members of the Trades Council remained independent Labour in their outlook, but there were comparatively few issues of political importance discussed; the Liberal minority was subdued after its crushing defeat of 1896, and there was little of that interplay of ideas between it and the independent Labour group which had so enlivened the debates of the earlier years. In particular, the new and less aggressive mood of the Council was expressed in an appreciable slackening-off of pressure to secure increased independent Labour representation in the Town Council: it was almost as if the Trades Council was giving up the attempt as hopeless. In 1895 and 1896 no fresh candidates for the Town Council were nominated by the Trades Council, though there was some reason for this in that several prominent Labour supporters were standing for re-election or were nominated by outside bodies: in the former year the Trades Council recommended workers to support Beveridge and Glass, and W. Cooper of the S.D.F.,

tax. Livingston had said of Mann that 'if he was to represent the views of the Aberdeen Independent Labour Party on the question of protection he was not the man to represent North Aberdeen' (*Daily Free Press*, 23 April 1896); but there is no evidence to suggest that Mann in any way supported protectionist views. Nor did he consider the eight-hour day as a final solution of the problem of unemployment. 'The reduction of the working hours would never absorb the unemployed. It might minimise the evil, temporarily, but there always remained the power of the employers whenever they chose to lock the door' (Speech by Mann in Aberdeen, quoted in *Daily Free Press*, 7 Nov. 1895).

and in the latter year similar support was recommended for
Johnston and Beveridge, and W. G. Smith of the S.D.F.[1]
In 1897 a joint conference of the Trades Council, I.L.P., and
S.D.F. decided to contest four Town Council wards, but in
fact only two candidates, Glass and Catto, were nominated;[2]
and in the two following years there were again no fresh
Trades Council candidates, the Council participating in the
elections merely to help to secure the re-election of Cooper
in 1898 and to support the unopposed return of Johnston
and Beveridge in 1899.[3]

This loss of interest in elections to the Town Council was
more apparent than real. It certainly did not mean that the
Trades Council was satisfied with the composition of the
Town Council or with the work done by it. True, the small
Labour group on the Town Council in the 'nineties continually put forward an advanced municipal policy upon
such questions as working-class housing and the employment
of a direct labour force, and scored some minor successes
along these lines; and the very existence of the group served
to keep the other members of the Town Council on their
toes. But the reforms carried through at the instigation of
the group were sometimes illusory, and this was particularly
so in connection with the 'fair wages' clause in Town Council
contracts.

The inclusion in contracts of a clause binding contractors
to pay their workers at not less than the standard rate of
wages approved by the trade unions concerned was from
the first one of the main objects of the Trades Council's
policy in relation to the Town Council. The incorporation
of such a clause in contracts was resolved upon by the Town
Council in December 1891; but there was a loophole in the
clause, which provided for special cases or exceptional

[1] *Minutes*, 23 Oct. 1895; *Daily Free Press*, 31 Oct. 1895; *Minutes*, 23 Sep. 1896.
Glass and Cooper were elected in 1895, and Johnston and Beveridge in 1896.
[2] *Daily Free Press*, 11 Sep. 1897. Catto was defeated, Glass re-elected
unopposed.
[3] As already noted, the Town Council elections of 1898 coincided with the
Parish Council elections, which were not neglected by the Trades Council or
the S.D.F.

circumstances, and in any case the resolution was rescinded within a month.[1] A year later, the Town Council again adopted the clause, this time without any apparent loophole, and it remained in force for the remainder of the decade in spite of attempts to modify it.[2] On the face of it, the Trades Council should have been satisfied with this, but in fact there were constant complaints of evasion of the clause, especially in connection with the contracts for coal and police clothing.

In 1895, the Trades Council resolved: 'That it is desirable in connection with the Town Council contracts that a clear definition of what is meant by the standard rate of wages, similar to what exists in the London School Board contracts, should be drawn up.'[3] This was not done, however, and disputes over the interpretation of the clause continued. The Town Council itself was by no means eager to enforce the stipulation, as it showed on one occasion in 1897 when it considered tenders for the coal contract. The lowest tender came from Ellis and M'Hardy, coal-merchants, but this firm had 'struck out the condition as to the payment of the standard rate of wages, explaining at the same time that they paid their men the standard rate of wages and more'. Nevertheless, the Town Council decided to accept this tender, rejecting an amendment to accept the next lowest tender instead.[4] A few years later, W. Johnston summed up the feelings of trade unionists on the 'fair wages' clause by saying that it 'was not worth the paper it was written upon. Every year there was some disagreement in connection with this police clothing contract.'[5]

---

[1] *Minutes of the Town Council of Aberdeen*, 7 Dec. 1891; 4 Jan. 1892.

[2] *Ibid.* 19 Dec. 1892. For attempts to modify the clause by providing for exceptional circumstances, see *ibid.* 5 Feb. 1894; 19 Mar. 1894. The Aberdeen School Board adopted a standard rate of wages clause for building contracts on 8 Oct. 1891.

[3] *Minutes*, 22 April 1895; 24 April 1895. The difficulty of definition was particularly evident in the case of those unskilled workers who had no trade union.

[4] *Minutes of the Town Council of Aberdeen*, 5 July 1897.

[5] *Minutes*, 6 Feb. 1901. The wording of the much disputed clause was as follows: 'It is hereby stipulated and declared that the successful offerer shall

Clearly, it was not lack of grievances needing to be remedied which accounted for the apparent decline of interest in Town Council elections on the part of the Trades Council in the late 'nineties. One obvious factor of great importance in this connection was the continued refusal of the Town Council to hold its meetings in the evenings instead of at three o'clock in the afternoon: as a consequence, very few working-men, if elected to the Council, would have been able to attend its meetings or those of its committees. On two occasions in 1893, and again in October 1894, Beveridge proposed that meetings of the Town Council and, where practicable, of its committees should be held in the evening, but his motions were narrowly defeated.[1] J. I. Mundie, a working-man who could not attend afternoon meetings, was then elected to the Town Council, and to meet this case Johnston, on 20 November 1894, proposed a very moderate motion that the meetings of three committees of the Council—on which committees Mundie was to sit—should be held in the evening for eight months of the year. But the motion was lost by thirteen votes to nineteen.[2] Nevertheless, Mundie refused to give up his seat; he succeeded in attending 13 out of 25 Council meetings, and 14 out of 42 committee meetings, during the municipal year 1894-5.[3]

At a Town Council meeting in December 1895, Johnston once more brought the matter up by proposing that Council meetings should be held at 7 p.m., and that committee meetings should also, as far as practicable, be held in the

be bound to pay the standard rate of wages relating to the particular trade to which his specification applies.' S. and B. Webb, *op. cit.* p. 399, state that by 1894, 150 local authorities in Britain had adopted some kind of 'fair wages' resolution: one wonders how many of them experienced difficulties similar to those in Aberdeen.

[1] *Minutes of the Town Council of Aberdeen*, 20 Feb. 1893; 10 Nov. 1893; 15 Oct. 1894.   [2] *Ibid.* 20 Nov. 1894.

[3] By comparison, Johnston who, as a full-time official of the Trades Council, did not suffer from disabilities similar to Mundie's, attended all 25 Town Council meetings, and 113 out of 141 committee meetings, during the same year.

evening. The previous question was moved as an amendment, and was lost; but a further amendment, which had the effect of deleting from the motion all reference to committee meetings, was carried on the casting vote of the Lord Provost.[1] Nevertheless, substantial victory seemed to have been won: Council meetings were to be held in the evening. But it was a short-lived victory, for a few months later the Town Council, over-riding a protest from the Trades Council, decided to rescind its resolution on this subject. The reasons advanced in this debate showed considerable thought, not to say ingenuity: there was said to have been frivolity at the evening meetings; serious business could not be dealt with at 'the fag-end of the day'; it was inconvenient for some members of the Council, who lived outside the city, to attend evening meetings; and it was unsatisfactory for a member of the Council—Mundie—to be present at Council meetings without having attended the committee meetings which led up to them. Not surprisingly, nobody suggested that it was desirable to exclude a working-man—and some professional men—from the Town Council.[2] Mundie had now had enough: he resigned his seat on the Town Council.

Once a year for the next four years, Cooper or Johnston proposed to the Town Council that its meetings should be held in the evening, but on each occasion the motion was lost.[3] Consequently, it was extremely difficult to find working-men who were willing to be nominated as candidates in Town Council elections. Thus, the joint committee of the Trades Council, I.L.P., and S.D.F. proposed to contest four seats in 1897, but only two candidates were nominated: Keir said that the joint committee had found it 'exceedingly difficult to find candidates willing to lose money by attending Town Council meetings'.[4] In the following year, when the Trades Council did not nominate any candidates, it

[1] *Minutes of the Town Council of Aberdeen*, 2 Dec. 1895.
[2] *Ibid.* 6 April 1896; *Daily Free Press*, 7 April 1896; *Minutes*, 25 Mar. 1896; 8 April 1896.
[3] *Minutes of the Town Council of Aberdeen*, 6 Nov. 1896; 5 Nov. 1897; 14 Nov. 1898; 10 Nov. 1899. Voting was close; e.g. 16 to 15 in 1898.
[4] *Daily Free Press*, 4 Nov. 1897.

13

nevertheless affirmed its 'conviction that the interests of labour will not be properly attended to until bona-fide labour representatives are allowed an opportunity of taking part in the deliberations of the Corporation's affairs'.[1] Probably the relatively greater participation by the Trades Council in elections to both School Board and Parish Council[2] was partly due to the fact that these bodies had already adopted the principle of holding their meetings, and those of their committees, in the evening. The Aberdeen School Board which held office from 1885 to 1888—the first Board which had any workers amongst its members—had initiated the practice, and the first Aberdeen Parish Council (1895-8) had followed the example; though, as a precautionary measure, the Trades Council continued to place the item concerning evening meetings in the forefront of its programmes for elections to these bodies.

Yet the barrier to working-class candidatures imposed by the Town Council's refusal to change the hour of its meetings did not wholly account for the decline in participation by the Trades Council in elections to that body in the late 'nineties. If suitable candidates could have been found, it seems likely that the strength of the Labour group on the Town Council could have been considerably increased: in the municipal year 1896-7, Beveridge, Cooper, Glass, and Johnston represented between them three separate wards, and it is reasonable to suppose that at least the other seats in those wards could have been won by Labour candidates. There was nothing to stop the Trades Council from forcing the issue of evening meetings by nominating a large number of working-class candidates: if

---

[1] *Minutes*, 5 Oct. 1898.

[2] In the School Board elections of 1897, the Trades Council nominated five candidates (and the S.D.F. one), but only one of these, Keir, was elected. The *Daily Free Press*, 17 April 1897, considered that the huge vote polled by the Rev. A. Webster (who stood as an independent candidate, with Trades Council support) had told adversely, through the cumulative voting system, on those of the Labour candidates. In 1900, four Trades Council candidates (and one S.D.F.) were nominated for the School Board: two of them, Keir and Duncan (together with Webster), were elected. The Parish Council elections of 1895 and 1898 have been referred to above.

those elected should prove too few to sway the balance in
the Town Council, then they could either resign their seats
or simply absent themselves from meetings until the issue was
faced. But such tactics were not adopted: they presupposed
a militant temper comparable to that which had prevailed
in the early 'nineties, and the mood of the Trades Council
and of the workers it represented had changed.

On one occasion in 1899, A. Robertson, addressing the
Trades Council as its president, dwelt at some length on the
causes of the comparative lack of interest in social questions
which, he considered, had been manifest in the previous
year or two in Labour organisations and in the Liberal and
Conservative parties. He believed that political factors were
partly responsible: the government in office was a strong
one and there was little likelihood of obtaining concessions
from it by means of pressure; and the newspapers were
diverting the attention of people from social questions by
talk of war. But there were other reasons:

'For a number of years back they had enjoyed an almost
unprecedented run of prosperity so far as trade was concerned, and it was an unfortunate fact that when such a
condition of affairs occurred people had not got the same
incentive to interest themselves in these matters. . . .
Locally they found that on a small scale exactly the same
thing had been happening. The hands of the clock, with
regard to labour affairs, had been put back. A few years ago,
when many of them were out of work, a great many things
were being done that were not heard of nowadays. They
were all discussing the question of the unemployed. . . .
Public boards did their utmost to alleviate the condition of
the workers, and relief works were started in every town,
Aberdeen included. The voice of the discontented working
classes had so much effect that evening meetings were
adopted at the Town Council and a standard rate of wages
was fixed. Immediately this run of prosperity came evening
meetings were thrown out, and now they were not very
particular about the standard rate of wages. . . .'[1]

[1] Report of Trades Council meeting, *Daily Free Press*, 14 Dec. 1899.

Robertson was an acute observer, and there was a good deal of truth in his remarks. It has already been noted that there was in Aberdeen a certain degree of correlation between 'good' years—years of booming economic conditions and relatively full employment—and periods of expansion of trade union membership and industrial activity: as, particularly, at the turn of the 'eighties and in the late 'nineties. Similarly, it is possible to establish a connection between 'bad' years and periods of abnormal political activity on the part of the Trades Council: as, notably, in the mid-'eighties and the early 'nineties. This latter connection was not as direct, in some cases, as might be expected. The effects of unemployment were not inevitably in the direction of a changed political outlook and a swing away from Liberalism: in the early 'nineties some of the metalworking craft unions in particular—ironmoulders, boilermakers, engineers—were badly affected by unemployment yet remained more or less Liberal or neutral in politics. Probably the element of leadership, the dominant position of such men as J. C. Thompson, was exceptionally important here, in conjunction with the powerful hold of traditional and established ideas over men's minds.

  Nevertheless, when all due allowance has been made for exceptions, the general rule is fairly well established: years which were good from an economic point of view were associated with trade union expansion, while less prosperous years saw much more emphasis by trade unionists on political activity. Political and industrial activity were, in fact, seen as alternative forms of expression, alternative means of achieving the same end: the maintenance and improvement of the conditions of workers. The industrial weapon was obviously of more value in periods of relatively full employment, though it was also brought into play, in a defensive sense, in less propitious times. Generally, however, a turn to politics, towards an application of pressure upon organs of government, was evident in periods of depression; and, naturally, the political weapon bulked larger in the armoury of those trade unions, mainly of unskilled or semi-skilled workers, whose industrial strength was never very great even when economic conditions were most favourable.

No sharp dividing line was drawn between political and industrial activity, greater emphasis being placed—by much the same group of trade union leaders—upon one or the other form of activity according to the circumstances prevailing at any particular time. One further point, of considerable importance, needs to be made in this connection. As has been shown, there was an expansion of trade unionism in Aberdeen in the late 'nineties which was comparable in some ways with that which had preceded it in the late 'eighties and early 'nineties; but the earlier period was distinguished in a qualitative sense by the fact that then, at the turn of the 'eighties, industrial activity on the part of the Trades Council coincided with political activity to produce a many-sided and vigorous development.

It is appropriate to conclude this account of trade unionism in Aberdeen by relating, rather by way of epilogue, the circumstances surrounding a revival of political interest in 1899-1900—a revival associated with a general election, the Boer War, and the S.D.F. It was apparent that in the late 'nineties the Aberdeen branch of the S.D.F. was increasing in strength and influence. It was beginning to stand out as early as 1895, when the Trades Council agreed to give a collectivist resolution precedence over the usual eight-hours one at the May Day demonstration: W. C. Mitchell protested rather weakly at this, and a joiners' delegate, who 'contended that the Trades Council was being made subsidiary to the Social Democratic Federation', moved that the collectivist resolution be not adopted, but he was defeated by a large majority.[1] In the next few years, there were several other pointers to the growing strength of the S.D.F., such as the election of W. Cooper to the Town

[1] *Daily Free Press*, 25 April 1895. The resolution in question was as follows: 'This meeting unites with the workers of the world in asserting the solidarity of the interests of labour, and pledges itself to support the emancipation of the people from the thraldom of capitalism and wage slavery, and for the realisation of collective ownership in the means of life.'

13 *

Council, and of W. G. Smith to the Parish Council in 1898
—Smith actually received more votes than another successful
candidate, Elrick, vice-president of the Trades Council, who
was standing in the same ward.[1]

The local S.D.F. also published a newspaper, *The Comet*,
which appeared at infrequent and irregular intervals. The
first number of this paper claimed considerable and widespread activity on the part of the organisation. 'We are
running propagandist meetings every Saturday in every
town within a twenty mile radius of the city. We are running
three meetings every Sunday in the city. . . . Our organisation is growing, our numbers are increasing, and we are out
with a paper with a name that explains erratic dates of
issue.'[2]

Confident in its new-found strength, the Aberdeen
S.D.F. decided, early in 1899, to adopt H. M. Hyndman as a
Labour candidate for North Aberdeen at the next General
Election. The party then made an approach to the Trades
Council, asking for its co-operation. Here, however, considerable opposition was met, not only from Liberals but
also from members of the Trades Council who were independent Labour supporters:[3] it was argued that the S.D.F.
had taken its decision as to a candidate without consulting
the Council, that there was no real chance of defeating the
sitting Liberal M.P., and that Hyndman would stand not
merely as a Labour candidate but also as a Socialist, with
the result that the Labour vote would be divided against
itself. The executive committee of the Trades Council
recommended that no action should be taken in the meantime, and when this was put as a motion against an amendment to co-operate with the S.D.F. in running Hyndman,
the Council divided evenly, thirty-three votes being cast on

---

[1] *Daily Free Press*, 2 Nov. 1898. Until a year or two before this, Elrick had
himself been a member of the S.D.F.

[2] *The Comet*, 25 June 1898 (in King's College Library, Aberdeen).

[3] There had been some ill-feeling between the I.L.P. and the S.D.F. over
candidatures for the Parish Council elections of 1895 and the Town Council
elections of the following year; Beveridge, in particular, was critical of the
S.D.F.

each side. The chairman, Robertson, then gave his casting vote in favour of the motion.[1]

Shortly after this, the Trades Council sent representatives to a conference to discuss local parliamentary representation, the other organisations represented at the conference being the local S.D.F., and a Social and Labour Committee (which seems to have consisted mainly of middle-class men who had been members of the now-defunct Aberdeen I.L.P.).[2] On 23 August 1899, the Trades Council considered two recommendations made by this conference. The first, that Cunninghame Graham should be asked to contest South Aberdeen at the next election, was adopted by sixty-one votes to three. The second, that Hyndman should be asked to contest North Aberdeen, was proposed, and the previous question was moved as an amendment. Once again the Trades Council divided evenly, motion and amendment each receiving thirty-six votes; and as before, the chairman gave his casting vote against Hyndman.[3]

The matter was at this unsatisfactory stage when the Boer War began. From the first, the Trades Council made no bones about its opposition to the war. A few days before fighting began, it resolved unanimously: 'That this Council strongly protests against the action of Her Majesty's Government in forcing on a war with the Transvaal Republic in the interests of Jewish and British speculators. . . .' In moving this resolution, Diack agreed that 'the Boers might have their evils, but he maintained whilst our own colonies were suffering from exactly the same evils Britain had no right to wage war in this case'.[4] In April 1900, the Trades Council accepted an invitation from the local S.D.F. to attend an anti-war meeting which was to be addressed by

[1] *Minutes*, 31 May 1899; 14 June 1899; 27 June 1899; *Daily Free Press*, 15 June 1899; 29 June 1899.

[2] See *Daily Free Press*, 10 Aug. 1899. Members of the S.D.F. were inclined to challenge the *bona fides*, as a Labour organisation, of this new group, saying that it was 'a body of gentlemen . . . but it was all so indefinite . . . '.

[3] *Minutes*, 23 Aug. 1899. As it transpired some time later, Cunninghame Graham was unwilling to contest South Aberdeen.

[4] *Daily Free Press*, 5 Oct. 1899; *Minutes*, 4 Oct. 1899.

Cronwright Schreiner; and the meeting was held in spite of attempts to break it up made by a howling mob of normally respectable citizens.[1]

When the 'khaki' election was held in the autumn of 1900, the Trades Council was caught unawares; it had not secured Labour candidates for either of the Aberdeen constituencies, and it therefore had to decide between the Liberal and Conservative candidates contesting both seats. The decision turned on the attitude of the candidates towards the war in South Africa. Both Conservative candidates supported the war wholeheartedly, but the two Liberals were much closer to the Council's standpoint on this question. The Trades Council was not entirely satisfied with the Liberals' attitude: it would have liked them to oppose annexation of the two Boer republics, and to be less equivocal in their public pronouncements.[2] Nevertheless, on 26 September 1900, the president of the Trades Council, Elrick, proposed 'that in view of the fact that no Labour candidates were standing, nor any pledged anti-annexationists, the working-classes should support both Liberal candidates'.[3] To Elrick 'Mr. Bryce was not just exactly the kind of candidate that he would place implicit confidence in as a Labour candidate. . . . At the same time, in view of the strong opposition put forward by the Council against the Government in connection with the South African question, there was only this one course open to them.' Other delegates spoke in the same vein. Diack, for example, said: 'It was entirely due to Mr. Bryce's attitude on the Imperial question that was before the country that they supported him on the present occasion . . . the present

---

[1] *Minutes*, 18 April 1900. The Rev. Webster made a telling point at the meeting by reminding the audience that in the time of Wallace 'Scotchmen were treated as Boers by the invading English'. Police kept the mob outside the meeting-hall at bay, and later in the evening troops were called out (*Daily Free Press*, 21 May 1900).

[2] The furthest Bryce went was to declare: 'I have never called the war unjust. . . . I have always called it unnecessary . . . both parties are in the wrong. . . . But I have condemned . . . and I shall continue to condemn the policy of the Ministry which landed us in war' (*Daily Free Press*, 26 Sep. 1900).   [3] *Minutes*, 26 Sep. 1900.

conflict was clearly between the peace party, on the one hand, and the war party on the other.'[1]

Elrick's motion was carried without opposition, and most members of the Trades Council then threw their energies into the campaign of the Liberal candidates, Bryce and Pirie, both of whom were successful in the election.[2] But at its first meeting after the poll, the Trades Council emphasised the special and temporary character of its support for Bryce and Pirie. Standing orders were suspended to enable a motion to be put: 'That our action in voting for the Liberal candidates as against the imperial policy of the Government in no way nullifies our oft-repeated resolution in declaring ourselves in favour of independent political action on the part of the workers of the city of Aberdeen.' The motion was agreed to:[3] for the last time, and for a special reason only, the Aberdeen United Trades Council had supported a Liberal parliamentary candidate.   The era of trade union support for the Liberal party had ended.

[1] *Daily Free Press*, 27 Sep. 1900.
[2] The Aberdeen branch of the S.D.F. decided to remain neutral and take no official action (*Daily Free Press*, 2 Oct. 1900).
[3] *Minutes*, 3 Oct. 1900.

APPENDIX

TABLE I

WEIGHT AND VALUE OF FISH LANDED AT ABERDEEN HARBOUR, 1887-1900

Year	Weight in cwt.	Value in £
1887	176,163	86,900
1888	181,317	101,941
1889	193,845	118,503
1890	252,247	169,120
1891	300,524	211,322
1892	355,603	236,273
1893	414,251	263,957
1894	472,152	277,365
1895	531,902	300,415
1896	592,703	335,882
1897	650,809	377,536
1898	756,896	445,781
1899	886,037	537,422
1900	974,633	617,928

Source: W. Pyper and others, *History of a Great Industry*, p. 18.

TABLE II

SHIPBUILDING IN ABERDEEN, 1880-1900

		Vessels launched		Vessels on hand	
Year	No.	Total tonnage		No.	Total tonnage
1880 .	7	7,990		5	4,600
1881 .	10	9,827		9	11,290
1882 .	7	9,673		13	10,740
1883 .	16	11,618		7	8,880
1884 .	7	7,651		6	5,610
1885 .	6	6,246		2	2,176
1886 .	1	1,550		3	3,450
1887 .	6	1,822		4	5,114
1888 .	9	6,440		9	9,110
1889 .	11	9,470		12	9,040
1890 .	15	9,228		13	9,970
1891 .	12	6,724		7	6,180
1892 .	13	3,414		6	3,060
1893 .	5	2,574		3	2,670
1894 .	12	6,875		4	1,055
1895 .	14	4,748		12	1,518
1896 .	19	5,075		13	6,391
1897 .	17	5,349		16	11,000
1898 .	28	9,175		29	14,005
1899 .	28	11,973		27	6,805
1900 .	32	6,905		10	2,657

Source: Daily Free Press, 13 Dec. 1894; 11 Dec. 1900.

TABLE III

PLANS OF DWELLING-HOUSES SANCTIONED BY ABERDEEN
TOWN COUNCIL, 1883-8[1]

Year (1 Dec.-30 Nov.)	Number of houses
1883-4	178
1884-5	157
1885-6	187
1886-7	208
1887-8	243
Total	973[2]

[1] *Daily Free Press*, 26 Oct. 1888. In time of depression, many houses the plans of which had been sanctioned would probably not be erected: in fairly good years, nearly all of them would be, as appears to have been the case in the 'eighties.

[2] These 973 houses were nearly all tenements, so that a commentator in the *Daily Free Press*, 26 Oct. 1888, felt justified in reckoning that provision had been made for about 4,860 tenants or families. He further estimated the average cost of each house as being about £900; adding the value of industrial building and house extensions and alterations, he thought 'it may safely be assumed that something approaching about a million of money has found its way into the property market' in the five years. Some old houses were demolished in connection with city improvement schemes in these years, but the number of these was said to be 'trifling' compared with the number of new houses built.

TABLE IV

NUMBER OF TRADE UNIONS, AND OF TRADE UNIONISTS, REPRESENTED AT ABERDEEN TRADES COUNCIL

Date	No. of unions represented	No. of members represented
1882[1]	12	—
1884[1]	24	—
Dec. 1889[2]	over 30	—
Dec. 1890[1]	33	—
Feb. 1891[3]	—	6,951
Dec. 1891[4]	36	—
Jan. 1894[5]	—	4,679
Dec. 1894[6]	38	5,746
Dec. 1895[6]	40	5,883
Dec. 1896[6]	40	6,286
Dec. 1897[6]	41	6,016
Dec. 1898[6]	36	7,811
Dec. 1899[7]	35	8,211
Dec. 1900[7]	37	8,041
Dec. 1900[8]	44	—

[1] *Daily Free Press*, 25 Dec. 1890.
[2] *Ibid.* 26 Dec. 1889.   [3] *Ibid.* 5 Feb. 1891.
[4] *Ibid.* 24 Dec. 1891.   [5] *Ibid.* 19 Jan. 1894.
[6] *Report of the Chief Labour Correspondent of the Board of Trade on Trade Unions in 1898* [C. 9443], pp. 204-5. H.C. 1899. XCII.
[7] *Report of the Chief Labour Correspondent of the Board of Trade on Trade Unions in 1900* [Cd. 733], pp. 202-3. H.C. 1901. LXXIV.
[8] *Daily Free Press*, 27 Dec. 1900.

TABLE V

INDICES OF CHANGES IN WAGE-RATES IN SEVEN TRADES IN ABERDEEN, 1870-1900[1]

(1880 = 100)

Year	Building masons	Monumental masons	Carpenters and joiners	Scavengers	Farm servants	Bakers	Seamen and firemen
1870	100	100	92	—	83	90	—
1871	100	100	92	—	94	90	—
1872	100	100	100	—	92	90	—
1873	108	108	108	—	104	90	—
1874	108	108	108	—	123	90	—
1875	115	117	117	—	119	90	—
1876	115	117	117	—	154	100	—
1877	115	117	125	100	146	100	114
1878	108	108	117	100	130	100	114
1879	100	100	100	100	96	100	100
1880	100	100	100	100	100	100	100
1881	100	100	100	100	100	100	100
1882	100	100	100	100	104	100	100
1883	100	100	100	100	106	100	100
1884	100	100	100	100	123	100	151
1885	100	100	100	100	109	100	114
1886	100	100	100	100	108	100	114
1887	100	100	100	100	98	100	114
1888	100	100	100	100	98	100	114
1889	100	100	100	103	100	100	157
1890	108	108	108	103	117	100	187
1891	108	108	113	103	115	100	173
1892	108	108	113	103	123	100	173
1893	108	108	125	103	119	100	160
1894	108	108	125	103	123	100	160
1895	108	108	125	103	135	100	160
1896	115	108	133	116	123	105	160
1897	115	108	133	116	125	114	173
1898	123	117	133	116	131	124	173
1899	130	117	138	116	131	124	173
1900	123	117	133	116	142	133	173

Table taken from G. Evans, *Trade Unionism and the Wage Level in Aberdeen between 1870 and 1920*. The index-number for any one year represents the highest rate received in that year.

INDEX

14